Songs of Life

SONGS of LIFE

The Meaning
of Country Music

> <

by Jennifer Lawler

ISBN 1–880654–09–1

Cover photograph courtesy of the House of Cash.

Black and white photography credits: Earl Gutnik pages 17, 94 and 129; all others courtesy of the Thomas Sims Archives. Drawings of country music performers which appear at chapter headings, originally contained in *Country Music Souvenir Album* (Denver: Heather Enterprises, 1968) are courtesy of Thurston Moore.

Contents

Acknowledgments

A number of people have contributed to this book, giving valuable suggestions and useful information, and to mention them all here would not be possible. Several persons in particular, however, merit special consideration. I would like to thank Junior O'Quinn, president of the Hank Williams fan club, for his help in answering questions about fan clubs, and for his quotes about Hank Williams, Sr. I would also like to thank David Bryant and Ted Cramer of WDAF-61 Country in Kansas City, Missouri, for their kindness in discussing the marketing of and audience for country music. In addition, the Country Music Foundation graciously opened its archives to allow me access to an extensive and useful collection of materials dealing with country music.

Special thanks are offered to Johnny Cash and the House of Cash for permission to use the cover photograph.

Our gratitude must also be conveyed to Thomas S. Sims who has a special love of country music and the numerous artifacts which it has generated. The great majority of the illustrations in this book were taken from his personal collection. The Thomas Sims Archives contains numerous and unique records, stage costumes, show posters, programs, magazines and books, as well as many photographs. Tom Sims periodically offers country music materials for sale, and interested collectors can request information from him, at P.O. Box 1464, Spring Valley, California, 91979, or from the publisher, Pogo Press.

Finally, I must thank my husband, Bret Kay, for great support, patience and encouragement, not to mention his exceptional research skills.

Without the help of all of these people, and many others, I doubt this book could have been completed on time and on target.

Jennifer Lawler
Lawrence, Kansas
September 25, 1995

Songs of Life

Introduction

This book considers why country music has become so popular, especially among people who have not traditionally identified with country music. The purpose of this book is to explore the meaning of country music to its listeners, but more importantly, to show that country music is important not simply as an aspect of popular culture or as a manifestation of folk culture, but as a literature in itself, worthy of serious study. While country music is often belittled and undervalued, it is, or can be, a true and beautiful expression of the human condition. Country music should be respected as an art form.

As a literature scholar who focuses on Old English poetry, which extends from about the sixth or seventh century to the eleventh, I have always appreciated the possibility of regarding folk song as art. The Old English poets and singers were skilled at constructing complex metrical forms, but their lyrics were most assuredly meant to evoke simple emotions. These poems appealed to many people and yet Old English scholars show that they are also the source of endless scholarly speculation and literary interpretation. When the speaker in the ancient poem "The Wanderer" asks, "Where has the steed gone?" he is not asking about a missing horse, but a missing time, a lost time. The Wanderer, a "walker alone," laments his exile from others. "There is not one to whom I dare plainly tell my heart," he says. These are simple emotions, simply expressed. Isolation and nostalgia are stated in simple enough terms for all to understand, yet the message is nonetheless complex. The steed is not merely a steed. Neither, in country music, is the bottle just a bottle nor the truck just a truck.

As a country music fan, I discovered after some time what should have been apparent from the first: what we call literature, and what we call country music, are intimately connected. Each can express human conflicts and emotions in a straightforward yet highly symbolic way. Thus, it seems to me, we owe country music the same consideration we owe to Old English and other poetry as well.

As a teacher and a scholar, I have always respected language and am impressed with the way it is used by country music songwriters. My experience as a commentator on literature and my background as a literature scholar should serve to illuminate the songs. While other writers have focused primarily on the culture of country music, (for instance, Curtis W. Ellison's *Country Music Culture*) or the themes of country music songs generally (for instance, Jimmie N. Rogers' *Country Music Message* and *Country*

❋

**Songs
of Life**

Music Message: Revisited), I will show the art of the music, as it were, using literary analysis (in a sense), to show the degree of sophistication and intelligence necessary for both writing and understanding country music lyrics.

The difficulty, of course, lies in overcoming resistance to such an idea. Country music is not regarded as a serious form of art, as literature. It is rarely taken seriously by anyone but the most devoted fans and the most dedicated performers. They have seen and understood the nature of what they are doing. For those who stand outside this circle, skepticism surely predominates.

The historical perception of the typical country music fan as a redneck, rural man who listens to extremist radio programs and right-wing Christian preachers while installing a gun rack in his hand-me-down American-made pickup truck, hound dog at his feet, wife barefoot, pregnant and of a doormat disposition is in fact a misperception. Though people who inhabit the backwater areas and are functionally illiterate may listen to country music, most of the audience do not fit this characterization. But the stereotype persists. For this reason, many fans of country music are closet fans. They don't announce their preference; they turn the radio off before answering the phone or the front door. At stop lights, they switch stations so people won't guess. In short, they listen to country music ashamedly, in secret. And this only helps to perpetuate the stereotype. But we shall see that the country music audience is increasingly diverse, that people who listen to country music are making an intelligent choice, that the country music message is more sophisticated than is usually thought, and that the message is one of interest to people from all walks of life.

In short, it's okay to come out of the closet now.

Country music has always suffered from an image problem. Elizabeth Peters' best-selling mystery of 1989, *Naked Once More,* is set in Appalachia. The main character makes up words to a country song: "My man done left me for another/So I turned to the arms of my ever-loving brother/I'm a low down sinner and so is he/ We'll fry in hell for eternity."[1] The character remarks that the song practically sings itself. The slightly obscene lyrics are amusing, but the joke only works if the reader believes such lyrics actually could exist in a country music song. And most readers are willing to believe.

Country music is considered simple and provincial, for the simple and the provincial. A new critical perspective—one that doesn't assume the stupidity or naïveté of country music and its audience—will show that country music is not for dummies. It requires life experience, intelligence and a detached sense of irony to appreciate country music and to become a whole-hearted fan.

The instruments have always been a vital part of country music. As one writer points out, if you have a steel guitar and a banjo, you can't produce anything but country music.[2] Yet the melodies themselves are not what is important. For the country music listener, the music lyrics are what is important, but they do not tell the whole story. The appeal of country music has its basis in other areas as well.

We will see how country music "works" by exploring its history, marketing, and audience, and by examining the songs written or chosen by select performers who, by singing about various themes, tell us about ourselves. These themes include love, living, social concerns, and women's issues. These themes and how they are rendered show that country music is, if nothing else, music about the lives of ordinary people. It is "vernacular" poetry, one might say. It reflects the society around it. Its themes are the themes of literature. S.A.J. Bradley, a scholar of Old English, in writing about ancient vernacular poetry, says that its themes "are serious matters of philosophy, the history and truths of the faith, public and private ethics and issues of social responsiblity."[3] Country music, no less than ancient literature, occupies itself with these timeless but always pressing human concerns. Unlike rock music, which is concerned with fantasies and dreams of things we will never have and things we will never be,[4] country music is concerned with a common human condition, with universal experiences that most of us, if we are honest, can identify with. But country music comes with its own coherent culture, and since this culture is often deeply traditional, country music has had difficulty changing and accepting change. "It takes five cowboys to change a light bulb," cowboy singer Red Steagall says, "One cowboy to change it and four others to reminisce about how good the old one was."[5]

For many years, country music was a regional music, an ethnic music, a music that spoke to the concerns of a small group of people. Country music performers came from small southern towns and grew up listening to the preacher and other country music performers from other small southern towns. They tended to focus on experiences specific to rural life and spiritual salvation.

The larger culture, which, of course, impinged on this smaller one, was often the focus of resentment. Its values did not always coincide with their values. While it celebrated material prosperity and corporate success, they saw poverty and hardship. The larger culture often dismissed them and their concerns as unworthy of attention. When attention was given, it was usually in the form of ridicule. While the larger culture glamorized city life, they understood the significance of country life. All of these tendencies of the larger culture went against the grain for those who identified with country music culture. Country music culture celebrated certain values and expected certain standards. Though this is changing, country music culture is still strongly rooted in a traditional milieu, and performers attack or leave that milieu at their own risk. Fans, while loyal, will abandon performers who do not appreciate the country music culture with all its attendant demands. Such demands are that performers remain humble and caring, that they not let fame or fortune change them, and that performers be aware of their role model status, and tread carefully. They must participate in and appreciate fan activities and must never forget who is the boss (either the fans or God, depending). They must open up their personal lives and be able to withstand intense though admiring scrutiny. Clearly, such demands can be overwhelming. Failing to meet these demands translates into failing one's fans. Such failure inevitably leads to a loss of fan support and once that support is lost, a country music career cannot continue. As an example, at the Country Music Association awards each year, winners always thank their fans, in contrast to pop or movie stars, who thank everyone except their fans.

The center of country music production is Nashville, Tennessee. There, a small cadre of agents, producers, and promoters controls the recording, production and distribution of almost all country music. While various performers such as Waylon Jennings and Willie Nelson have attempted to eliminate this stranglehold by recording in other cities such as Austin, Texas, or by using non-country producers, none has been markedly successful in challenging the authority of the country music structure in Nashville. In other musical styles, one can pursue a music career in a number of different cities. Alternative rock bands have successfully recorded in Seattle, Washington, as well as Minneapolis, Minnesota and other cities, not just in New York or Los Angeles. To be a country music singer of any stature and reputation at all, one must go to Nashville. This reinforces the country music culture and tends to limit the direction that country music takes; it also increases competition among performers. The most aggressive may make it, the most talented don't necessarily succeed.

Nonetheless, the country music performer can shape the culture that has shaped him or her. Once a popular record is cut, the performer commands much more power than before, since the competition among producers and record companies is also fierce. As performers acknowledge wider varieties of influence than ever, country music expands. Country music performers have also begun to come from various walks of life. They are no longer primarily the rural poor. Newer stars such as Suzy Bogguss and Mary Chapin Carpenter have college degrees. Their education, as well as their social class background, is very different from what is perceived as typical among country music performers. Yet they are successful at country music, and have helped make positive changes. These performers bring new ideas and new attitudes to country music. They confirm the point that to sing country music, all that is essential is "a song and a guitar and a message to tell."[6] Country music performers respond and interact with the larger culture in more positive ways as well. As Bill C. Malone says, country music "has been consistently reflective and representative of the society which nourished it and of the changes in that society."[7] Country music, then, has become an intelligent, ever-changing commentary on important social issues of the day. Though it is commonly considered simplistic, escapist music, country music songs present ways to cope with human concerns, not to escape from those concerns.

These concerns are the "material" of country music. As songwriter Billy Sherrill says, "I think lyrics are damn near what country music is all about. Melodies are very easy to come by if you have a good idea and a good set of lyrics."[8] The primary concern for the country music songwriter is communicating a message. Other forms of music may focus on catchy melodies, but country music focuses on the message. Hank Mills, another songwriter, says, "Ideas are a dime a dozen. I could sit here for ten minutes and come up with ten good ideas for a song. The idea for a song comes from the mind, but the song comes from the heart—that's my concise definition of country music the way it is today."[9] Loretta Lynn explains, "I think all women get upset when they think some other woman is messin' with their husband or their man. I try to write everyday living, everyday life."[10] This is not to say that what is everyday is necessarily simple. Betsy Bowden, in her study of performed literature, remarks on "how complex are the ideas and expressions of ordinary people."[11] The effectiveness of a country music song depends on the clever selection of words and phrases and the construction of multiple meanings in the lyrics.

Because performers such as Loretta Lynn write many of their own songs, audiences perceive songs as being "about" the singer, as though songs are personal or are in some sense autobiographical. A case in point is Johnny Cash and his signature song, "Folsom Prison Blues." This song has convinced many fans that the Man in Black has spent time in prison, that the lyrics somehow form a true story about him, that it reflects an experience Cash has had. Even when the country music performer is not the songwriter, he or she often shapes, appropriates, the song. The singer may interpret the words differently from the original, or may even change the words to suit him or herself. Thus, songs can be made personal by the singer. For instance, Gary Burr wrote the popular song, "I Think About Elvis." When Patty Loveless wanted to record it, she asked him to make several changes since she was uncomfortable with some of the lyrics. He says, "Patty would rather not sing about hand guns and red meat. So I rewrote it and tried to get in touch with my feminine side."[12] In doing so, he transformed references to hand guns and red meat into references to hairdos, the late show and even the creature from the Black Lagoon. Not all are necessarily feminine references, but they were nonetheless much more acceptable to Patty Loveless. In the seventies, Tom T. Hall's "Harper Valley PTA" underwent an important change when Jeannie C. Riley changed "that" to "my." The song, "What'll You Do About Me?" underwent similar changes; the line "I'm on the porch with a two by two" was altered by a later artist to become "I'm on the porch with dinner for two," presumably to reflect the latter artist's belief in non-violence. If the audience feels the singer is being dishonest—that is, that the song has nothing to do with the singer—they feel betrayed and will express disappointment with the singer's lack of sincerity.

The audience connects with the country music performer intimately—as if they were the performer's family. The word "family" is often used by country music performers to describe their fans. This warmth and sense of belonging has helped spread the popularity of country music and has made its appeal more national—and indeed, universal. Country music, if it were once a regional or southern brand of music, is no longer so. The touring itineraries of three of the country music performers discussed in this book are worth looking at here. Hank Williams, Jr., for instance, in a one month period (June 1995) was expected to perform in the Midwest (Dayton, Ohio), as well as the Northeast (Camden, New Jersey and Boston) in addition to the traditional region (Lexington, Kentucky and Nashville). Tanya Tucker, in the same month, performed in Denver and St. Louis, places that are not historically considered strongholds of rednecks. Mary Chapin Carpenter's touring schedule for the same time period reflects the international appeal of country music. She planned to appear in Glasgow, Scotland and Vancouver, British Columbia. She also sang at the alternative rock capital of the world, Washington State, plus Sacramento and San Diego, as well as Telluride and Morrison, Colorado. She visited Hampton, Virginia, which is in traditional country music territory and Chattanooga, Tennessee, which is a town that likes its country music hard core.

Even a non-traditional area like Chicago celebrates a new-found attraction for country music. There, a major country music festival has been held annually since 1990. Country music performers sing with the symphony and the mayor sponsors the festivities. Other such festivals are held throughout the country, even in some of the unlikeliest places, including Colorado, Indiana, and Florida.

That country music is riding a huge wave of popularity is without question. Though the Grand Ole Opry, in the heart of country music culture, celebrated its 70th anniversary in 1995, it is much more recently that country music has been established as a viable form of entertainment in other parts of the country. But beyond that, why is country music worth our attention? As S.A.J. Bradley says about ancient vernacular poetry: "The poetry has an abiding relevance and what may be fairly called a nobility of purpose. It shows a deep awareness of the integrity and worth of the individual and of organized human society—as well as human concern for their tragic frailty."[13] If this is true of an ancient vernacular poetry, it is equally true of a modern vernacular poetry. Country music is literature and for that reason is worth study, but just as importantly, it has a cultural and social influence of great impact. Country music is worth examining in light of its importance to an enormous group of people. Such an examination will help to pinpoint and describe the culture and the audience of country music and will also highlight the intellectual challenges inherent in country music. The following pages will show that country music is not for dummies.

The History of Country Music

The history of country music reveals that country music is guided by a preoccupation with the past rooted in a milieu and a culture that embraces the traditional. Change has always come slowly and often painfully to country music. Even so, country music reflects the society around it, offering a secular alternative to personal troubles. It is the tension between tradition and change that is the creative force behind this brand of music, constantly pushing and pulling it in different directions. New singers and songwriters attempt to create new visions by using the traditional elements of country music, because they are deeply concerned with keeping country music identifiably country music. This concern with origins has helped country music weather many storms that have threatened and submerged other forms of music. This music celebrates shared experiences and a shared identity, though it sometimes makes unwarranted assumptions about those experiences and that identity. That is, not all people, not all fans, have the same experiences or beliefs. The performer must appeal to a common identity without assuming too much about that identity. Such assumptions risk alienating the audience, which is what happened, for instance, with Hank Williams, Jr.'s Desert Storm song, which no one really was in the mood for, and even K.T. Oslin's song "Younger Men," which explicitly referred to the inability of older men to perform sexually. Nonetheless, if a country music performer creates a controversy within the country music culture, a dialogue will almost inevitably ensue. If, for instance, a performer sings a song that alienates a listener, the listener will explain his or her point of view (on the radio, in a country music magazine, in a fan club newsletter). Sometimes a performer will explain his or her point of view about a given controversy. In this way, what is acceptable to country music culture is constantly under negotiation. A performer may "lose" the argument and suffer for it, but such sanctions are ordinarily arrived at only after a certain period of consideration by fans and country music executives alike.

Themes and Sources

Though often considered conservative, country music manages to reach out and appeal to countless listeners of all shapes, sizes, ages and political creeds. The themes of country music are the themes of literature: war, peace, growing old, loneliness, discrimination, love, dying. Country music is also about dancing and drinking and fighting. It dwells lovingly on the pleasures of the flesh. It is composed of splinter elements—folk music and gospel music, protest music and western swing, honky tonk and bluegrass, southern rock and Appalachian and even a new style called alternative country, which blends the melodies of alternative rock with the lyrics of country music. Country music has been influenced by spirituals and Mexican corridos, by singing cowboys and musical mountaineers. It has been celebrated in books and movies, and in Thomas Hart Benton's painting, "The Sources of Country Music" (1975), commissioned by the Country Music Foundation for its Hall of Fame and Museum in Nashville. But regardless of the names people have given its sources and its influences, it is country music, and its origins are in traditional British folk songs, brought over from that island centuries ago.

The traditional British folk song, especially the ballad, is the original source of American country music. Folk music, narrowly defined, is music that lives in an oral tradition and is learned "by ear." Folk music has a tendency to change as it passes from one person to the next. Each person who sings the song may develop his or her own version. Such ballads were sung, composed, revised and modified to suit the contemporary circumstances of countless poets. "Barbara Allen" is one folk song still sung today, but there are many others. "The Streets of Laredo" started life as "One Morning in May," a very old folk song. Variations on folk song themes also continue to suit contemporary tastes. The old folk song "All For The Love Of A Man" expresses a complaint theme common among country music love songs.

Instruments

The instruments used in country music may vary from none to many, but some important ones include the guitar, the banjo, and the fiddle; the harmonica and the accordion, which give country music a distinctive sound; the piano, the drums, and the electric bass, which are recent additions. Horns have been added to give country music a more "lush" sound. The mandolin, the dulcimer and the autoharp have also found their way into the hands of country music performers, and live performances are almost always amplified now, with an occasional acoustical performance to showcase the artist's vocal talent.

The poor folk of the South made music as entertainment, to while away the long winter evenings or to celebrate life's special events. In a traditional folk society, music is necessary in rituals and festivals. Songs are used to give news and information and often serve as a way for young people to learn about their culture. In modern times, such music fosters solidarity in a social group. It is not odd, then, that country music performers are considered "troubadours," and that country music performers, who often emphasize loss and longing, are called "tragic troubadours."

The connection between ancient folk and modern country music is made clear in Paul Hemphill's wry commentary:

> The ballads were sometimes based on castle slander ('Everything's OK on the LBJ'?), military exploits ('Are There Angels in Korea'?), or unusual occurences ('Carroll County Accident'?). With the coming of Christianity, some of the ballads took on a moralistic tone ('It Wasn't God Who Made Honky Tonk Angels'?).[14]

The rural south, because of its isolation and conservatism, maintained a folk music much longer than the rest of the country. This music was "discovered" and capitalized on early in the 20th century.

This oral culture—people composing new ballads or singing old ones—eventually became the equivalent of a literary culture. It became written when music publishers published the sheet music and record producers recorded the songs. In the 1920s, radio stations and record producers began to tap into the wellspring of country music. From the beginning, country music was populated by performers who were not real "hillbillies," and whose acts were based on the city dweller's perception of rural life, rather than being based on the actualities of rural life. Even so, many country music performers were real "hillbillies" and their acts captured the authentic music of the rural south. Thus, country music has always, though not obviously, been sung by people both with and without strong rural roots. Also, even from the beginning, there was opposition to the music on aesthetic grounds, in particular the non-standard language and dialects that characterized early country music. Ralph Peer, who produced music for Okeh Records, called Fiddlin' John Carson "pluperfect awful," though later sales changed his mind.[15] While much of the music might have been primitive and unsophisticated, the objections probably stemmed more from a lack of familiarity with the music than anything else.

Jimmie Rodgers and the Carter Family were among the first country artists to be widely known and are therefore considered influential in shaping the direction country music first took. Rodgers sang a blues-inspired country music while the Carter Family sang traditional Appalachian music. They relied on direct borrowing, re–composition, and original creation to compose the material—just as oral music has traditionally been composed.

Radio and Barn Dances

By 1922, radio station WSB in Atlanta was featuring the performances of country music fiddlers and singers. The audience response was overwhelming. The following year, WBAP, a station in Fort Worth, played square dance music on one program and the station was deluged with approving phone calls and letters. This enthusiastic response led to the programming of regular country music shows. In 1925, the Grand

Calendars were traditional ways to advertise country music. Two early sponsors of the Grand Ole Opry, Martha White Flour and Fortune Feeds, are credited on this 1950 calendar.

*Promotional photograph, circa 1948, of Purina's Saturday evening production of Grand
Ole Opry. This radio program originated on Nashville's WSM.*

Ole Opry made its debut as a radio program called "The WSM Barn Dance," broadcast
from its home in Nashville.

Such "barn dance" radio programs grew in popularity. They idealized family and
were marketed as family "get-togethers." Country performers often referred to their
co-workers as family (and still do), and there were numerous singing family groups.
Many performers took family relationship names, such as "Grandpa" Jones, and
"Cousin" Minnie Pearl. The country music performer has an immediate family, which
may be seen to include other performers, plus an extended fan family. This "family"
nature of country music culture, which is still extremely important today, stems partly
from the barn dance shows. Almost all country stars who began their careers in the
thirties achieved fame through these radio barn dances, including performers such as
Gene Autry, Roy Acuff, Kitty Wells and others.[16] Many of these barn dances were produced and broadcast locally, and each Saturday night, families would gather around
the radio and listen to the music. "Louisiana Hayride" is probably one of the best
known of the locally and regionally produced barn dances, but there were many others, such as KSTP's "Sunset Valley Barn Dance" in Minnesota, which ran for years, and
Kentucky's "Renfro Valley Barn Dance."

The station which perfected the barn dance format was Chicago's WLS, named for

Sears Roebuck, the "World's Largest Store." The show was "The National Barn Dance," which debuted on April 19, 1924. In 1933, this was the first country program to be broadcast coast to coast. Such shows featured a reassuring atmosphere and celebrated rural culture, a soothing combination during the days of the Depression. Performers would sing, talk about themselves and their songs, hawk products, introduce one another and generally present a casual atmosphere of music and conversation. The barn dances which were later telecast had dance segments where one could watch different dancers perform to the music.

The Grand Ole Opry went on to become the most prestigious of the barn dance programs, as well as the longest running. The sense of family is still strong. Performers on stage at the Grand Ole Opry still say they feel as if they have joined a family. The Grand Ole Opry is held in awe by aspiring singers. To be invited to play there is an honor and a privilege, though it pays very little; to be invited to join is the pinnacle of one's success. The Grand Ole Opry stands for the country music culture, for all the traditions of country music. It is a concrete link between the past and the present, between fans and artists. It is an institution to be upheld. It has been referred to in both admiration and disgust as the Mother Church of Country Music.

The Grand Ole Opry, since it is still essentially a radio program, is presented in segments. Each segment may have a particular host, such as Roy Acuff or Porter Wagoner, or it may have a particular sponsor, such as the Country Music Foundation, or it may have a particular theme, such as gospel music or Appalachian music. The show is comprised of performances, jokes, skits, and the like, while the audience waits, patiently and politely, through delays as taped advertisments are played or stage bands are changed.

Considered rustic and perhaps primitive, country music did not at first seem to have commercial possibilities. It was, of course, these commercial possibilities that made country music "written," in the sense that a record did not change. A song written by a performer began to stay essentially the same through many performances, although country music still retains much plasticity in this regard. Just recently, for instance, a country music singer in concert added an impromptu verse to a song that had been cut and produced and had sold millions of copies. This impromptu version was promptly recorded, cut, and produced. It sold, if not millions, a respectable number of copies. The alteration of lyrics is part of the performer-audience interaction. The audience doesn't want or expect the live performance to be the same as the recorded one. This is in direct contrast to rock concerts, which often make use of pre-recorded or dubbed material. Indeed, for the pop and rock fan, the preference is for the live performance to mimic the recorded one. So while commercialization limited the flexibility and plasticity of country music, it did not eliminate these characteristics entirely.

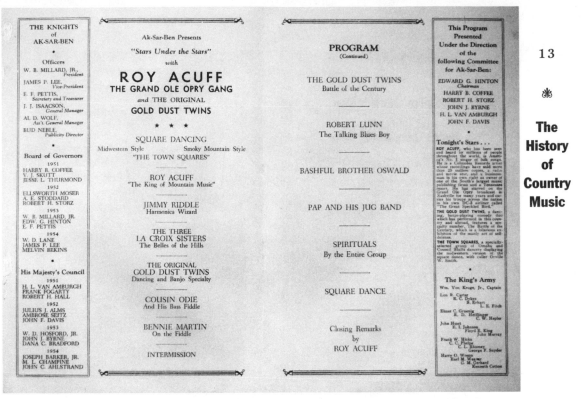

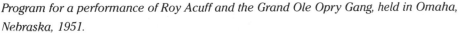

Program for a performance of Roy Acuff and the Grand Ole Opry Gang, held in Omaha, Nebraska, 1951.

The success of country music radio programs soon led to the production of country music records. Though records had been made in the early twenties, they became truly successful commercially only after radio programs brought people's attention to country music. By the late twenties and early thirties, country music recordings were multiplying swiftly on labels such as Okeh Records, RCA, MGM and others. The Depression, however, soon brought an end to such rapidly increasing country music record sales. The common feeling seemed to be, "Why pay for music when you can hear it on the radio for free?" Partly because of this, WSM formed a booking agency in 1933 to help artists find live venues.[17] After World War II, three engineers from WSM started Castle Recording Company, the first commercial recording company in Nashville, which became a very important studio in the country music industry's early years.

The Grand Ole Opry

By the mid 1930s, radio had become the voice of country music. Instrumentals had been the dominant mode of expression at first. Fiddlers and pickers impressed the radio audience with their skill. But that changed when a banjo player called Uncle

From the late 1940s through the 1960s the Jimmie Skinner Music Center was a major national outlet for country music records. This record jacket carries its advertisement.

Dave Macon took his place on the Grand Ole Opry program. Just as important as his picking was his singing. Many of his songs were traditional ballads sung by laborers in the mines, the docks and the railroads of the South. The subject—social protest—was the subtle thread that held these ballads together, and made them a unified country music. Much of this early country music celebrated religious fundamentalism, the sadness of life on earth, and ethnic bigotry against non-whites and non-Christians. Soon, however, love came to be the dominant subject matter of country music; Roy Acuff, Gene Autry and Tex Ritter, among others, made this theme funny, touching and memorable.

Other themes included the transience of human life, and the conditions of labor. An anti-establishment populism is often at work; for example, the song "Take This Job

Record companies provide a variety of promotional pieces to retailers, ranging from this relatively small 1963 Decca Records display featuring Kitty Wells, to full size cardboard cutouts of the performers.

*Zeke Clements and his band were Grand Ole Opry cast members in the late 1930s. He is
shown with his "Bronco Busters" band during a 1962 WENO radio performance.*

and Shove It" never fails to get an audience yelling. Individual worth, rugged individualism and patriotism are celebrated as "country ethics," the values that country
music culture holds dear. Being an "outlaw," a prisoner, a wanderer—an exile from society—is a commonly expressed condition. Performers sing of these situations from
different perspectives. A performer might express a feeling, imagine a better life, escape from a situation, endure a problem. This sometimes takes the form of tension between "us" and "them." "They" are powerful and cruel; "we" are good. Country music
sets forth clear themes and familiar struggles. The performer and his or her fans are
on the same side. This is not to say that comic songs and novelty tunes have no place
here. Unrelieved seriousness is not valued. The performer is expected to exhibit a
sense of humor or rowdiness on occasion, and even a song with a serious intent will
often reflect a singer-songwriter's sense of the absurdity of the universe. One of the
best known and best loved country music singers who focused on comic tunes was
Roger Miller, elected posthumously to the Hall of Fame in 1995. "King of the Road" is
probably his most famous song, but he also recorded "You Can't Rollerskate In A Buf-
falo Herd," and "Dang Me."

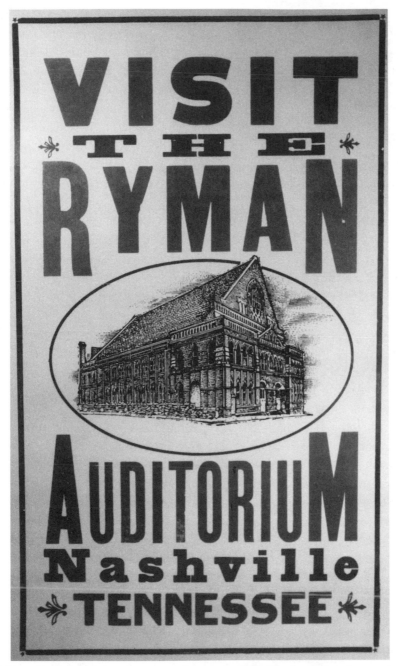

Hatch Show Print, located on Broadway Avenue in Nashville, has printed concert posters since 1879. Featured is the Ryman Auditorium which was the long-time home of Grand Ole Opry.

While radio became, and is still, the dominant venue of country music, television programming has also led to greater visibility for country music performers. The Grand Ole Opry's shows, for instance, have been broadcast on television for many years. Some country music performers have hosted their own shows, including Glen Campbell, Jimmie Dean, Tennessee Ernie Ford, Dolly Parton and Johnny Cash.

The Opry has remained important in the construction of a country music singing career. To this day, the Opry is a special place. Fans harbor life-long dreams of attending the Opry; singers have life-long dreams of performing there. Its move to its present location brought the usual doom saying, but the Opry is as strong as ever. The Ryman Auditorium, which many people considered the first and best home of the Grand Ole Opry was actually its fifth location. In 1943, the Grand Ole Opry moved to the Ryman and remained there for thirty-one years, long enough to establish a strong tradition. This tradition led to dissent among artists and fans when the Grand Ole Opry moved to its present location at Opryland, an amusement park just outside of Nashville. While the Ryman had excellent acoustics, its deteriorating condition and small seating capacity prompted the move. Though the Opry has been in its present location for over twenty years, many performers and fans still mourn the move. After the Ryman was renovated in 1990, many artists took the opportunity to perform there or to record there. Still, the Grand Ole Opry remains the country music performer's ultimate goal, no matter where it is located. Though much of the music performed at the Grand Ole Opry is extremely traditional in nature, most country music performers, even those branching out into new territory, do not feel they have truly made it until they have been asked to sing at the Opry. To be asked to "join" the Opry, that is, to become a member, a regular star, instead of merely a guest performer, is seen by many as a benediction and a blessing for their careers and the music they are performing.

By the 1940s, country music had garnered a wide audience, and singers such as Hank Williams, Patsy Cline and Lefty Frizzell became household names. It gained momentum during World War II, when it was broadcast over the Armed Forces Radio Network. Country music stars also joined USO tours to entertain the troops. The fans and the music industry began increasingly to focus on the star, the performer, with whom the audience identified.

The Nashville Sound

What is called The "Nashville Sound" emerged during the late forties. It was a smoother, more pop-sounding style of country music. One of its leading stars was Patsy Cline (once she was convinced to give up her hayseed image). The Nashville Sound relied on smoother production values and orchestration using violins instead of fiddles, and mellower vocals, without the characteristic dialect, nasal twang or yodel that had previously marked country music.

Country music developed a large following during the 1940s and 1950s. It also became more sophisticated. Instead of comprising only ballads or narrative songs—what John Hartford, a singer and songwriter, calls "word-movies"—the corpus began to expand.[18] Soon, what might be called lyric poetry made its appearance. Some consider Hank Williams' "I'm So Lonesome I Could Cry," the first well-known example of this. The short, fourteen line song (which looks remarkably like a sonnet) is not a ballad. It isn't even narrative. Through metaphor and imagery, it expresses an abstract idea, that of loneliness. Williams writes, "Hear that lonesome whippoorwill/He sounds too blue to fly," and "The silence of a falling star/Lights up a purple sky." These images illuminate the emotional state of the narrator, but there is no real narrative voice, since there is little narrative, merely imagery and metaphor.

Other writers followed in Williams' footsteps. Though the ballad is still the dominant form of country music, the lyric poem is not far behind in popularity. The ballad tells a story, with a beginning, a middle and an end, while the lyric tries to capture a moment, an emotion or a mood. The lyric tends to supersede the ballad in technique, sophistication and creativity; it is here that country music poets are most original.

For many years after Hank Williams' untimely death on New Year's Day, 1953, country music purists felt that those who did not emulate his approach and his sound were somehow doing violence to the country music tradition. Such a preoccupation with tradition and the past is, of course, of paramount importance to country music; it is one of the characteristics that separates country music from other kinds of music. It can even be said to define country music.

Style Changes in the 1960s

Nonetheless, in the 1960s, singers such as Waylon Jennings and Willie Nelson felt that one could sing differently from Hank Williams while still maintaining the country music tradition. One way this difference has emerged has been through the melding of blues and country. Simply put, blues and country music are both about hard times; therefore, they seem made for each other. They had, in fact, been blended together as far back as the 1920s, when Jimmie Rodgers sang blues-inspired country music for a radio station in Asheville, North Carolina. Still, it was only after some years that this connection was rediscovered and acted upon, and singers like Waylon Jennings met some resistance at first, for the music didn't sound exactly like country music.

Bluegrass

"Bluegrass," a form of country music which relies on virtuoso fiddle and banjo playing, with picking and runs designed to evoke an ecstatic response from the audience, also came of age during this period. Ideally, bluegrass needs a live audience. Reels and hoedown numbers are characteristic of bluegrass. It is a form of music that descends from Scots and Irish folk songs and dances. Bluegrass emphasizes individual performances and showmanship; bluegrass, these days, is essentially entertaining and escapist, meant as a release. Most songs are supposed to be happy and fun, instead of offering a message or a commentary.

Mountain Music

Mountain music was the forerunner of bluegrass. Mountain music, often called Appalachian music, reflects on hard times and is mostly in ballad form, telling of tragedies and unrequited love. Not necessarily meant only for entertainment, such music was an outlet; it also expressed emotion and, instead of escape, provided hard-headed directives on coping. In the mountains of Appalachia, the folk songs of England endured for centuries without major change. Mountain music makers say, "We're just home folks, and we don't want our lives—or our music—to change."[19] They still sing songs handed down from their Scottish and Irish ancestors. As one writer puts it, "The hill people still revere the traditions of their ancestors—self-reliance, hard work and the simple pleasure of music."[20] Nonetheless, each singer changes the words, creating variations on a theme. The purpose of Appalachian music is to reflect reality; therefore, it is a suitable vehicle for social and political issues. It is not surprising, then, that the country music influenced by Appalachian music has a strong tradition of protest, starting with coal-camp songs and working up to Vietnam protest songs. The Depression, Industrialization, World War II, Urbanization and the Civil Rights Movement have all produced corresponding songs. More recently there have been Desert Storm and Big Government protest songs.

Earlier Appalachian music was more fatalistic in the sense that one bore what trials one had to; this patient fatalism eventually gave way to angry, active songs. By the early 1960s, country music poets were as comfortable protesting social or political wrongs as any college student might have been. Many country music songs expressed support for unions and decried corporate attitudes which reduced humans to mere workers. And yet, a corresponding patriotic impulse not to criticize one's country is apparent in country music as well. This creates a tension between two strong traditions, a tension of which country music artists and fans are well aware.

The Singing Cowboys

These Appalachian music performers had counterparts in the singing cowboys of the 1930s and 1940s, with performers such as Roy Rogers combining western elements (horse riding, cowboy hat wearing) with country music. Singers such as Gene Autry, Tex Ritter and Roy Rogers acted and sang in movies often referred to as "horse op-

TOPHAND

MAGAZINE

VOL. 1—No. 3   HOLLYWOOD, CALIF.   JUNE 1946

ROY ROGERS

REPUBLIC PICTURES STAR

Roy Rogers' route to stardom as a singing cowboy led from the Sons of the Pioneers in the 1930s to films of his own and television shows in the 1940s and 1950s. Here he is featured on the cover of Tophand Magazine, *1946.*

eras." Others achieved popularity primarily through radio airplay and record sales. The cowboy (or cowgirl) image helped give country music a more national appeal and tied it in with the romantic nature of the west. The success of the cowboy singers led other singers and their fans to wear the Stetsons, the jeans, fringed shirts and dresses and the boots.

Cajun Music

Cajun music, originally a form of French Canadian folk music, influenced country music to add the use of the accordion. The Grand Ole Opry has a Cajun-style country music singer in the person of Jimmy C. Newman and Cajun Country, his band. Cajun music was recorded as early as 1928 and Cajun-inspired performers, mostly from Louisiana, still sing today.

Western Swing and Honky Tonk

In the 1940s, western swing expanded to widen the base of country music. Swing bands used as many as two dozen instruments (and even the drums once disliked by the Grand Ole Opry) to create an orchestrated sound. They played all over the country. Bands such as Bob Wills and His Texas Playboys combined jazz, blues and Mexican music into a broadly appealing sound. Western swing bands were meant to be danced to, and could be found in dance halls and ballrooms. This contrasted with honky tonk music, best epitomized by Hank Williams, Sr. This was hard-edged country, raw and emotional, meant for listening, not for dancing. It originated in Texas, and combined a western-based music with country music. The honky tonk sound emphasized hard living and bad luck. The name derives from the small, seedy bars where such music could be heard on the jukebox.

Rockabilly

Rockabilly emerged as a combination of black and white musical traditions in the South. Elvis Presley is the best known performer of this rock and country blend. During the 1940s and 1950s country music was being shaped by and was shaping other brands of musical styles.

Protest and Folk Music of the 1960s

A long-lived tendency towards conservatism pervaded the areas where country music was dominant. Some historians have attempted to show that country music was not acceptable to northerners who had idealized versions of folk, but even in the north, polkas and other forms of country music had faithful followers. Country music did not appeal to upper class southerners who thought it undermined their efforts to create "culture" and "refinement," especially in the center of country music: Nashville, the

Athens of the South. The conservatism of country music led to an interesting dualism: a protest tradition and an anti-protest tradition in the same genre. The upheavals of the 1960s angered many of the fans of country music and many of the writers as well, who felt that they and their families had struggled through hard times. It was difficult for them to appreciate the civil rights movement for minorities and women. They felt life had been just as bad for everyone all around and had little regard for what they saw as unjustified complaints.

Other, younger, singers, however, were more adaptable and more willing to see and criticize the flaws in the system. By the 1960s, folk music—the music of Bob Dylan and Joan Baez—had broken off (or been forced away) from traditional country music. Folk performers began to see themselves as different from country music performers and began playing in places country music performers did not—Woodstock, political rallies, and the like. Soon fans of one could not very easily be fans of the other. Much country music was conservative and reactionary (for example, Merle Haggard's "Okie from Musgokee"). But folk and country had the same heritage; it was merely the politics that were different. The split was political; the content of a song determined whether it was considered folk or country, not the characteristics, the tradition or the spirit of the song.

Country music, while peculiarly American, had, at this time, much input from Canadian folk singers and songwriters. The folk songs of Canada were perhaps idealistic and romantic, but they were not songs of protest. The political situation in Canada was much different (simpler in some ways); the songs were about people, not politics. These Canadian folk songs eventually helped bridge the gap between folk and country in American music. For this reason, it is today possible to hear the folk songs of American singers such as Mary Chapin Carpenter on every country music station; she is one of the biggest selling female vocalists in country music. The Country Music Foundation Archives accepts the folk singers Bob Dylan and Joan Baez as country music singers, though country music fans are less likely to consider them as such.

By the 1960s, such traditional country music singers as Johnny Cash, Kitty Wells and Waylon Jennings had recorded the songs of folk music writers such as Gordon Lightfoot and Bob Dylan. Soon folk singers were returning the favor. Bob Dylan's *Nashville Skyline* album was a breakthrough for country music, because an avowed folk singer had acknowledged the importance of country music and exposed a wider audience to it. Other performers began recording songs in Nashville and appearing on country music radio and television programs. One important television program was "Hee Haw," a barn dance program which idealized rural community and ran from 1969 to 1992.

Johnny Cash is perhaps the best known singer to benefit from this combination of folk and country traditions. In the late 1960s and early 1970s especially, he had a pro-

Cowboy boots of Lou Millet, circa 1963. Millet was a country and rockabilly singer and lyrics writer, who often performed in Baton Rouge, Louisiana.

found influence on country music. His born-again Christianity is a hallmark of country music; such faith is constantly explored and expressed in country music, even by those best known for living hard. Johnny Cash, during this time, was equally at home singing protest songs, giving free concerts in prisons and appearing on Billy Graham's television show. For Cash, there was no contradiction between a good spiritual and a good prison song. Somehow it all fit together. Cash was among those country music artists who never felt alienated from the singers of protest songs—in fact, he and Bob Dylan were friends even during the bitterest days of the "split" between folk and country music, when the politics of each could be identified respectively as "left" or "right." Cash saw no reason why one could not sing about the bad things in America as well as the good. He managed to appeal to the rugged individualism dear to the country music fan's heart, as well as maintain a sense of justice and compassion that led him to protest many conditions and situations in America. He could not be claimed by any political group, which was one reason for his great popularity.

Cash hosted a popular television program during the 1970s and it was through him that many folk singers were able to reach an audience. He was proud to introduce folk singers to country music fans—folk singers like Judy Collins and, of course, Bob Dylan.

This reunion of country music and folk music allowed the emergence of a new group of writers—Kris Kristofferson among them—who blended the sophisticated lyrical techniques of folk music with the deceptive simplicity of country music. A pivotal figure, Kris Kristofferson and his songs broadened the audience for country music and influenced its direction. By appealing to a more youthful and intellectual crowd, writers such as Kristofferson were able to challenge the general perception of country music as backwoodsy and rustic. Still, many country music fans resisted such music, feeling it did not fit the tradition of country music. Nonetheless, most singers and songwriters felt that country music was still doing what it had always been doing, only better. Much of the music of this time—early to mid 1970s—still retained the feel of traditional British folk ballads.

The 1970s and Anti-Protest Songs

By the mid 1970s the militant anti-protest writers, those responsible for such songs as "Okie from Muskogee" and "Where Have All the Heroes Gone?" had begun to mellow. In fact, Bill Anderson, the writer of "Where Have All the Heroes Gone?" admits to wincing every time he hears his song on the radio, which isn't too often anymore.

The broadening of the country music audience is also owing to the broadening of the experience that audience has. As James C. Cobb says, "The nation that embraced country music in the 1970s had been deeply affected by the twin shocks of defeat and disillusionment, traumas previously associated only with the experience and heritage of the southern states."[21] Additionally, economic prosperity put the South and southern lifestyles in a more respectable light. In 1961, only 80 all-country radio stations existed in the US; by the mid 1970s, they numbered over 1,000. By 1991, one-quarter of all radio stations were country, and in 1992, three of the top ten music acts were country. Country music is based on certain assumptions and a certain sense of identity; as those assumptions and that identity grows more open, the audience for country music grows as well. Even traditional country music fans are increasingly sophisticated; they have become better educated and more widely traveled and perhaps because of this, a little more tolerant of change in country music, though cultural gaps still exist, especially between newfound and traditional fans.

Women and Minorities in 1970s Country Music

In the mid 1970s, another change came to country music. African-American singers and songwriters joined the predominantly white cast of characters. Gospel music in particular has always had a strong African-American connection, as much of it stems from traditional spirituals. These spirituals often became the basis for blues and Motown music, but they also have a strong affinity for country music. Ray Charles is one who clearly understands the relationship of blues and country; his music explores this relationship. Even more mainstream African-American singers appealed to the country music audience. In 1973, Charley Pride, the first African-American to break into country music big, earned more money than any other singer in the history of country music. The following year, 1974, The Pointer Sisters' song, "FairyTale," made the top of the country charts. Gladys Knight and Joe Simon have recorded country music in their own distinct styles. More recently, Cleve Francis has also achieved acclaim. The Black Country Music Association tries to help open doors for African-American singers, songwriters, and producers.

Nonetheless, the success of African-American singers and song writers has not always been accepted. As in any other sphere of economic activity, racism and sexism have run rampant in the country music industry, though that is changing (slowly, painfully). These days, the vast majority of singers and fans are still white, but more and more African-Americans are finding a place.

Women have met with a little more success in country music. The male singing stars still dominate, with women and groups achieving less acclaim. There have always been some successful female acts, Patsy Cline being a notable example, though there are still few successful female songwriters. As women's roles in society have changed, so, too, have their roles in country music. At first, women sang as members of groups, as did the women of the Carter Family. Then, they began singing as duos, with male partners. (The best known pairs are George Jones and Tammy Wynette, Dolly Parton and Porter Wagoner, and Loretta Lynn and Conway Twitty.) Finally, women graduated to solo acts. As women have gained more independence in society, they have taken more important roles in country music as they have done in other musical styles such as folk and rock.

Many of the most successful female country music artists began their careers in the late 1960s and early 1970s, including Dolly Parton and Loretta Lynn. These two made their names with realistic, down-to-earth story-songs that were especially appealing to women who could perhaps more easily identify with these women than with traditional country music singers. The increase in female entertainers led to a corresponding increase in the audience for country music. Dolly Parton, of course, is known for her exaggerated personality, even by non-country music fans. It was a number of years before she was taken seriously as a singer and a songwriter, perhaps because her outrageously feminine presence distracted people. A core following has always been committed and faithful to Parton, and as the years go by, that following

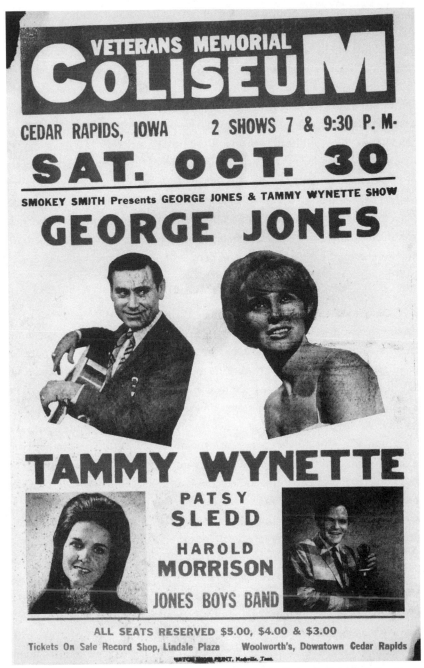

George Jones and Tammy Wynette were a popular duo before, during, and after their brief marriage. This Iowa show poster dates from 1967, early in their concert tours.

increases. Her songs have been sung by such artists as Linda Ronstadt and Emmylou Harris, both of whom have had many crossover hits. The seventies were the right time for the hard-hitting, sexually suggestive or controversial songs that these women sang, including Tammy Wynette's "D-I-V-O-R-C-E" and Loretta Lynn's "The Pill" and "One's On the Way." Many of these songs can be likened to the protest songs of the 1960s; they are women's protest songs.

Of course, the male side of country music responded with songs about the place of women. The ugliest of these is probably Johnny Paycheck's "All American Man." That women are made for men's use is the message of this song, and it is a message that underlies much country music, but this is slowly evolving. Younger singers and songwriters describe more balanced and equal relationships and women continue to grow as a force in country music. Just as the growth of country music has accompanied significant social and economic change, country music has been an agent for social change, communicating, as it does, to people of all kinds.

Gospel Music

The 1970s also saw an increase in gospel music, so much so that it has become its own genre, where once it was merely a variety of country music. Gospel music is fundamentalist and direct. In gospel music groups of singers create intricate harmonies. Though most of the hellfire has subsided, its message is still basic. Jesus saves, family values will carry one through. Gospel music is considered a separate genre of music these days, yet its influence on country music is great. Almost all country music singers have recorded a gospel song or two. Many country songs have a gospel message—something about the discovery of Jesus or faith in God. This kind of country music appeals most to the traditional country music audience, though the younger and more diverse members of the audience also appreciate these concerns. Country music theology is fairly simple and straightforward and has not evolved too much in the last century. It is cautiously optimistic; not only is God around and caring for you, but after death, there's a happy future somewhere. A new genre, Christian country music, is an off-shoot of gospel, though it is really the product of promoters and not of genuine demand or interest. It has not taken off as a viable style of music and seems doomed to mediocrity with little radio play. Fans who are interested in religious messages tend to turn to gospel music, the more authentic sibling of country music.

Many secular, mainstream country music writers are beginning to grapple with the problems of faith. However, these problems belie the simplicity of country music religious beliefs. Both Dolly Parton and Larry Gatlin have written songs dealing with the difficulties of leading a good Christian life. These qualities are part of many country music songs.

Some of the appeal of country music is in that basic message; much of the audience is concerned with returning to their roots and re-establishing some of those traditional values represented in country music. Yet country music also, as Reba McEntire has pointed out, allows the listener "three minutes of rebellion." Country music consists of simple messages that are easily underestimated. Writers are fond of clever phrasing and work to create an emotional response in the listener. Ambiguity is popular in the music, as in life. As one critic points out, "Country music holds no attraction for those who do not want to be reminded of where they come from, where they are, or where they are likely to be going."[22] By the mid to late 1970s, the audience for country music had grown to include members of the counter-culture, former rock fans a little disillusioned with rock sentiments and lifestyles, and college students who liked the sound of the music. Then, too, there remained the usual rednecks and good ol' boys who had always been the staunchest fans—and severest critics—of country music.

Influences of the 1970s

Although country music has been slow to change, the 1970s were the era of great upheavals. Then, country music was subject to the not-so-benign influence of rock music. One brand of country music, known as southern rock, is a hybrid of blues, bluegrass and rock. Such singers as Elvis Presley, Carl Perkins and Johnny Cash started out blending country and rock in what became known as rockabilly; all had audiences that consisted of country as well as rock fans, but Perkins could also boast blues fans. However, rock soon took a different direction, with Elvis following it, and country music went elsewhere. Southern rock, especially as now performed by such groups as the Charlie Daniels Band, appreciates loud volume but also appreciates the techniques of traditional country, especially of the fiddle-picking variety. Southern rock relies on a peculiar blend of country, blues and rock values and lifestyles. It celebrates the long-haired country boy who might smoke pot. But it also stresses rugged individualism and the live-and-let-live defiance characteristic of traditional country music. Southern rock is preoccupied with its roots, with the past, but it is also always new and experimental.

The 1970s were an era when barriers crumbled and in no arena was this more so than in country music. While rock took on a country sound, the distinctions between country music and "pop" music were disappearing. Dozens of songs hit both the country and the pop charts, thus ensuring more and more mainstream attention to country music. During this period, country music concert promotion became one of the fastest growing segments of the music industry. By the early 1980s, performers who were accustomed to singing in night clubs and honky tonks were filling concert halls and amphitheaters. From the traditional venue of the small hall, honky tonk bar or country nightclub, country music acts took over some of the biggest stages in the country, including football stadiums and college auditoriums. Throughout the 1980s and early 1990s, such concerts were huge money-makers for the artists and promoters. Concerts generate the most income for country music performers—and always have. Country music performances have displaced the mega-concerts of the rock-oriented seventies, which indicates an audience of immense proportions.

Country music has influenced an odd variety of performers. The hard rock group Lynryd Skynryd recorded a version of Rodgers' "T for Texas." Johnny Cash sings on a U2 compact disc. The Eagles are considered country and, in 1994, a collection of country music stars created a tribute album to them. In 1995, the album *Come Together: America Salutes the Beatles,* with singers such as Tanya Tucker, Kris Kristofferson and Suzy Bogguss covering Beatles' hits, debuted at number 11 on the country charts, after Garth Brooks (*Hits,* #2) and before Reba McEntire (*Read My Mind,* #20). Tony Bennett, Patti Page, Bing Crosby and Phil Harris belong to earlier generations of singers whose hits were covers of country music songs.

The influences on country music have grown much as the audience has grown. When country music was an isolated phenomenon, with singers and writers expressing themselves as their families had done for generations before them, a certain purity of sound was possible to identify and maintain. But as musical, social, political and artistic influences increase and change, so, too, will country music, though its fans and poets might not like the fact. Still, most acknowledge that the trend is irreversible—and some even go on to propose that perhaps this isn't such a bad thing. However, many writers and performers express an unwillingness to let country music lose its identity.

The 1980s and the 1990s

During the 1980s, this concern was especially apparent as more and more songs and singers crossed over, easily moving from pop to country and back. Yet something curious happened in the late 1980s: pop music essentially disappeared. The soft rock sound as performed by artists like Barry Manilow, Duran Duran, and others lost audience and appeal. Radio stations and record producers turned to "newer" sounds, and pop singers and songwriters were absorbed by alternative music, by hard rock or by country music. This "disappearance" of pop music added thousands of listeners to country music as popular music radio stations went to country music formats and singers and songwriters accepted the label of "country" for themselves. The heavily-promoted urban rap music did not appeal to all listeners. Mainstream teenagers and young adults turned to country music as an alternative. Unfortunately, this in turn caused pop and urban programmers to try their hands at country music programming, which means people who know little about country music program it and must rely on chart hits to make up their play lists, ignoring unusual or older country music artists.

This disintegration of pop music, a tried-and-true genre, led to changes in country music, which became more commercialized and polished (or "slick" as its detractors say). In fact, it began to sound an awful lot like the pop music it replaced, with smoother vocals and more complicated melodies. During this period, partly in response to this polish, there emerged a version of country music that attempted to recreate the honky tonk sound of Hank Williams. This return to the traditional honky tonk sound was spearheaded by Williams' son, Hank Williams, Jr. Two kinds of country music now exist simultaneously: "old style" and "new style." Old style is considered the more traditional of the two and the new style is thought to be more experimental. The singers who epitomize the new style, the "young hats" as they are called, are criticized for all looking and sounding much the same. Some groups, such as the good ol' boys who make up Sawyer Brown, manage to bridge both styles, celebrating the old honky tonk style but embracing the new as well, deftly blending the two.

While some country music performers consider themselves traditional and others consider themselves progressive, they share the same basic audience, with some exceptions. Hard-core fans tend to side with the old style; brand new fans tend to prefer the new style. But in the main, old and new style draw from the same audience, are played in the same clubs, are heard on the same radio stations and are danced to by the same people. Country music line dancing is another phenomenon that attests to the huge popularity of country music. No geographical or age boundaries exist. More than a thousand country dance clubs exist in the U.S., with more opening every day. These have caused marketing executives to see a bigger market. Many artists release songs that have a dance remix.

Performers are awarded Country Music Association awards and Academy of Country Music awards as well as Music City News Country Awards. Such awards programs, televised live like the Oscars and Emmys for film and television, were established to honor country music singers, since at one time country music singers did not win Grammys. Winners of various categories have included everyone from Ricky Van Shelton to Garth Brooks and include now-obscure performers such as Johnny Bush (1969—Most Promising Male Artist) and Susan Raye (1970 and 1971—Most Promising Female Artist). Performers such as Olivia Newton-John have also been the "people's choice," much to the chagrin of the established country music culture in Nashville, since she was not perceived as a "true" country music singer. More recently, Billy Ray Cyrus has been a fan favorite who has received little respect from either older performers or the music industry. Such awards productions generate interest in country music and also show how large the audience actually is.

✳

**Songs
of Life**

Strong female vocalists are also beginning to dominate the scene. Now more than ever, women such as Reba McEntire command huge sums of money for appearances and have large followings of the faithful. Country music has come a long way, in some respects. In others, it is the same as it was in 1925, when the Grand Ole Opry first hit the airwaves.

The Marketing of Country Music

According to the Country Music Association, country music record sales grew 13% from 1994 to 1995 and have more than doubled since 1990. Country music record sales alone have reached $2 billion annually.[23] This does not include concerts, radio and television advertising revenue or country music magazine circulation. These numbers indicate the economic power of the industry, as well as the popularity of the music.

There have been many factors suggested to explain this phenomenal growth. The appeal of the performers, and the lack of competition from other forms of music, as well as other reasons might be given, but much credit is owed to marketing efforts that are more successful than ever before. Country music and country music performers are promoted everywhere. Country music is responsible for much tourism, both to Nashville, the heart of the country music industry, but also to Branson, Missouri, where such stars as Charley Pride, Glen Campbell, Mel Tillis, Mickey Gilley, Roy Clark and even the Osmonds appear in theatres named for them. Wax museums, car museums and halls of fame appeal to the fan as well. Country music festivals attract fans from all over the region or country. The best known of these is Fan Fair, held in Nashville each summer, but other festivals take place in locales such as Detroit Lakes in Minnesota or the Ozark region in Missouri. Rodeos offer opportunities for fans and performers to gather; some singers perform solely on the rodeo circuit and manage to make a successful living that way. State fairs also provide ample opportunity for performers to sing. At the Minnesota State Fair in 1995, of nine grandstand concerts, six were headlined by country music performers. The organizer said she preferred working with country music performers, for they knew their schedules months in advance and could confirm play dates quickly. She also admired other evidence of their control over details. Such methodical organization is not characteristic of other forms of music.

In addition, country music has its own literary production. Biographies, autobiographies, histories of country music and photographic encyclopedias are published by mainstream as well as specialized presses. Over 200 books covering some aspect of country music were in print in 1994, when Dolly Parton released her autobiography, *My Life and Other Unfinished Business*. She followed in the footsteps of Johnny Cash, Loretta Lynn and Hank Williams, Jr., among others. Patsy Cline has been the subject of numerous biographies, even well into the 1990s. Plays and the 1985 film

33

Sweet Dreams (starring Jessica Lange) used Cline's brief life to make a dramatic story. Country music novels have also been written, including James Lee Burke's *The Lost Get-Back Boogie* (1986) and Thomas Cobb's *Crazy Heart* (1987). Fan publications and numerous country music magazines, such as *Country Music, Music City News,* and *Country Song Roundup* can be found on newsstands. Academic journals devoted to the scholarly study of country music performers and their art include *The Journal of Country Music* and *Journal of the American Academy for the Preservation of Old Time Country Music.* Academic conferences are also organized, including The Annual Country Music Conference, hosted by Mississippi State University. Such serious attention to country music broadens the audience and the market for country music. Some of these scholars have the stated goal of preserving old-time music, while others are more concerned with documenting manifestations of popular culture. The study of country music as popular culture has received serious attention in recent years, even though the first "Elvis conference," hosted by the University of Mississippi at Oxford, provoked surprise, ridicule and jeers. Country music archives exist throughout the country, often on university campuses, dedicated to preserving the artifacts and music of the country music culture. Nonetheless, most of these scholars still approach country music as simply a form of popular culture, without addressing the literary merit inherent in the music.

Country music is marketed in other ways as well. It is a theme for cruises, where guests can meet their favorite performers and listen to them in small, intimate concerts. Country music singers have long appeared at state fair grandstand concerts and they now include the Native American casinos as indoor concert sites.

Country music is sold through a variety of venues, including recordings, music videos, radio, and live performances. Even Wal-Mart sponsors country music acts by having free parking lot concerts with as many as three thousand fans showing up to listen. Magazines profile the stars, fan clubs celebrate them, clothing and memorabilia bring an aspect of the star into the fan's home. Fans who collect country music memorabilia save everything from ticket stubs and programs to key chains and matchbook covers. Fans will often limit their collection to one performer, or one style of music (for instance, bluegrass or honky tonk). Each year, a national convention brings together this huge network of buyers and sellers of country music memorabilia.

Because country music has been marketed and promoted so well to people of great differences, its appeal has become almost universal. Garth Brooks, for instance, has sold over 30 million records and CDs. In Ireland, where he received a "Best Country Act" from the Irish Recorded Music Awards, he has sold more than 500,000 records to date, which shows the worldwide appeal of country music and country music per-

RUSTIC
RHYTHM

ℛℛ K

A Unique "Brand" Magazine For A Country-Brand Audience

May 1957   35c

Readers of Rustic Rhythm *didn't need a label to recognize Faron Young on this 1957 magazine cover.*

*Other promotional ways to wear the name of a favorite performer were record-shaped
keychains and lapel buttons.*

formers. A new product will also promote country music—Country Vid Grid, an
interactive CD-ROM of country music performers' videos.

Other formats promote country music and country music performers as well.
Country music performers have always had close ties with the television and movie

industries. The Nashville Network (TNN) on cable is entirely devoted to programs featuring country music performers, shows about performers and all aspects of the country music culture. Ties between the music and screen industries extend back many years. Westerns and "hillbilly" movies were popular from the late twenties to the forties. In the 1950s and 1960s, singing cowboys such as Roy Acuff, Roy Rogers and Gene Autry were movie stars. Later country music stars such as Kris Kristofferson starred in more mainstream fare. He was portrayed as a sex symbol rather than a singer. In 1980, two important movies bolstered interest in country music. These were *Urban Cowboy,* a fictional account of a blue collar couple who entertained themselves in the country music culture way, through drinking and dancing at honky tonks, and *Coal Miner's Daughter,* based on Loretta Lynn's autobiography. More recently, George Strait has appeared in *Pure Country* (1992) though this movie did little to generate interest in country music. Those who watched the movie were already country music — and specifically, George Strait — fans.

Country music stars create film personas that usually remain the same. George Strait will never play a villain or a lawyer. He'll always play a good ol' boy with his heart in the right place. Like the singing cowboys, such country music performers are still expected to sing. If they don't sing as part of their roles, they will record a movie soundtrack album. Other country music movies attempt to explore the culture and myth of the tragic troubadour. *Honkytonk Man* (1982) finds that music itself can save the performer bent on self-destruction, and *Tender Mercies* (1983) shows how music, love and gospel songs can save an alcoholic singer.

In addition, country music is marketed at theme parks. This not only includes Opryland, which houses the Grand Ole Opry as well as other concert venues, but Tennessee's other theme park, Dollywood. Performers have opened "homes" and museums dedicated to maximizing their visibility and marketability. Loretta Lynn's ranch is open to fans, Twitty City is visited by thousands each year, and the House of Cash attracts many fans, too. Barbara Mandrell and others operate museums-cum-gift shops in Nashville and other cities. The Gene Autry Western Heritage Museum in Los Angeles is filled with rooms displaying western clothing, lunch boxes, and bedding featuring the cowboy actors. There are also museums celebrating Jimmie Rodgers and Roy Rogers, the latter boasting a stuffed Trigger. Other museums dedicated to country music in general are located throughout the country. The Country Music Foundation's Museum and Hall of Fame, located in Music Row in Nashville, Tennessee, was established in 1967 and attracts about 350,000 visitors annually. It has an extensive collection of costumes, instruments and other memorabilia. With sixteen permanent exhibits, several changing displays and the actual Hall of Fame, it is a veritable history of country music. The exhibits document different branches of country music, including rockabilly, honky tonk and others, plus provide information concerning song-

Performance dress of Marge Linville Warren, cast member of Town Hall Party, a 1950's country music television program. The dress was made by Nudie's Rodeo Tailor, Nudnick Cohen, proprietor. Nudie Cohen of Hollywood created the rhinestone cowboy look and made costumes for many of country music's stars.

writers and performers. The Hall of Fame also offers archives for researchers, as well as educational programs. The Country Music Foundation, which operates the Hall of Fame, has a press that publishes material of interest, including republications of historical documents and Hatch Show Print posters.

Other marketing efforts exploit fans' memories of their performers. These are the reunion tours that are popular in all areas of music. In country music, the reunion tour of Tammy Wynette and George Jones, conducted in the summer of 1995, seemed to emphasize the memory of past performances. These two, former partners and formerly married, now past their prime, were expected to provide interesting sparks because of their well-known love-hate relationship. These tours and recordings rely on the willingness of fans to pay for nostalgia.

Country music performers have discovered that they can not only market themselves, but because they are models for their fans, modeling gender roles, marriage and family, loving and success, they can generate sales for other products. That is, they also model consumption and can often dictate trends in material consumption.

Thus, country music performers are tapped to vouch for non-country music products. QVC, the cable home shopping network, which suffers an image problem just as country music has, is working in conjunction with country music star Clint Black to expand the appeal of QVC to consumers who think it is "not for people like me." Clint Black has also appeared on some packages of Keeblers' Wheatables; his favorite part of the deal, he says, is the commercial he shot with Ernie the Elf.[24] Other country music performers have caught the attention of marketers, who say they want to connect their products and services to the back-to-the-basics image of country music. Reba McEntire, for example, appeared on packages of Fritos and has boosted sales for Frito-Lay by 40% since 1994. The group Alabama is promoting a new line of food products called "Alabama Country Hits." These country hits include vegetable soup and chicken with dumplings, among others. For several years prunes have been the sweet in Barbara Mandrell's cookie jar as she does television commercials on behalf of Sunsweet Pitted Prunes. Singer Trisha Yearwood, who has a degree in music business, promotes Discover Card, which donates money to scholarship funds. While endorsing products is not new for country music performers, the great success of these efforts and the significant sums of money paid to the singers are new.

Corporate sponsorship of tours has long been a feature of the music business, with companies such as Marlboro, Jim Beam, Crown Royal, and Miller Lite promoting stars in exchange for certain advertising rights.[25] Some performers don't care to be associated with alcohol and tobacco products, however, and their needs have been answered recently by corporate sponsors such as Fruit of the Loom or Chevrolet.

Corporate sponsorship of tours helps both sponsor and performer. Each uses the other to achieve greater name recognition. "Country music is hot," says one marketing firm, "It reaches some prime demographics, the target consumers." Many women, aged 25–40, listen to country music; this group does an enormous amount of buying for families.

Such successes in marketing and promoting country music, and the association of country music performers with other products has increased the recognition of country music beyond other types of music. It is almost impossible to imagine Mick Jagger on a bag of Fritos and it is equally impossible to imagine Frito-Lay wanting him there. The wholesome image of country music works to its advantage during marketing and promotional opportunities. These, and other strategies, ensure continued interest in country music and reaffirm the connection of country music with mainstream culture.

The Audience for Country Music

For the country music fan, the relationship with a performer can be quite intimate. Fans are considered "extended" family by most country music performers. Live performances by country music stars help maintain this rapport with the audience. Even humorist Erma Bombeck was awed by the connection country music performers have with their fans. In one column, she wrote: "Most marriages should be as exciting, compelling and lasting as the one between country singers and their fans. Those who sit out in the darkness give them loyalty, forgiveness, love and admiration. Those in the spotlight give it right back."[26]

The country music performer appeals to the fan for many reasons, including a willingness to meet with fans. It is not unusual for singers to go out to meet the busses of tourists who make their way to Branson, Missouri, or to Nashville, Tennessee. Country music performers tend to be fans of other country music performers. Singer Tim McGraw stood in line with everyone else to get singer Lorrie Morgan's autograph at Fan Fair.[27] Country music performers, too, don't tend to have social aspirations. They don't need to join the country club. This keeps them close to their audience. Or at least, it helps their audience to perceive them as being close, as not getting above themselves, forgetting where they came from, or who got them there. "Country singers (with a few exceptions) are known for treating their audience with respect and warmth, by singing to them, not at them, and by spending as much time as possible talking to them after a performance,"[28] says one country music critic.

At the Grand Ole Opry, where former President George Bush and his wife put in an appearance in 1985, and President Richard Nixon came to its grand opening in 1974, fans talk with the stars on stage, receive autographs and take snapshots. This informality is apparent at other venues as well. In exchange for the support of the fan, the country music performer is expected to be authentic. His or her personal life must somehow reflect the public performance. Personal sincerity is expected, though rowdiness can relieve the seriousness of such an image. For the audience to identify most fully, the lyrics, which are more important than the melody or the instruments, must reflect realistic depictions of life. The words and feelings must sound as though they came spontaneously from the singer.

The performer is best appreciated if he or she is a poor boy/girl made good. It is difficult for a fan to hear a singer sing of poverty and hard times if the singer is known

41

to lack such experience. Fans want to believe that the singer understands their troubles, and they want to see that country music artists are ordinary people who have been affected by the same forces and situations that affect the fans. Even the late baseball great, Mickey Mantle, found this appealing. His favorite song, Roy Clark recalls, was "Yesterday When I Was Young," and he often asked Clark to sing it at various gatherings. A few years before his death, Mantle wrote to Clark and said,"Hang in there. I want to hear 'Yesterday When I Was Young,' at my funeral." In August of 1995, he did.[29]

Many country music performers, such as Hank Williams (both father and son), Ernest Tubb, Dolly Parton, Loretta Lynn, have written their own songs to capture this authenticity. As singer/songwriter Kim Richey says, "I don't believe in all up-tempo, positive songs because life isn't like that. Country music is about real things happening to real people."[30] The task of the country music songwriter is complicated. For all that the songs seem simple, they can be difficult to write. As David Ball says, "They say great songs are not written—they're rewritten."[31]

In addition to writing their songs, many performers try to produce them, instead of allowing others to do so. This allows them to maintain creative control over their work and over the final product that is distributed to the consumer. Since they will be held responsible by their fans regardless of the actual amount of control they had, country music performers have sought to gain greater control over the industry. In other words, they are seizing the means of production. Country music marxism, as it has been called.

Each performer is expected to stand for something, to have a social conscience. This is evident in the charitable programs organized by country music performers, including Farm Aid, local food banks and relief for the victims of the Oklahoma City bombing. But performers are also expected to "believe" in something, whether it is patriotism, the environment, or women's rights. In this way, the fan can appreciate a larger goal or concern than merely listening to "feel good" music. The fan can become part of a larger community in this way. Community is an important point of identification for the country music fan.

Country music performers affect the emotional state of the audience members by interacting with them, by creating a feeling of family. The audience feels a sense of community with the star but fans also feel community with each other, as groups of fans band together to seek out and share information about the star.

The interaction of fan and star is one important reason for the widespread appeal of country music. The idea that country music is the province of beer-swilling hog farmers alone is a misconception. Its appeal crosses gender, professional and income lines. In fact, even in the early 1970s, *Billboard* magazine published a study that showed that country music fans had the highest income levels of all music fans, thus drawing from high socio-economic classes.[32] Even in Alaska, country music performers are able to sell out concerts. The state of Indiana had its first country music expo in 1995. As a respite from thoughts of crime the O.J. Simpson jurors requested country music recordings such as Garth Brooks' *Hits* during their year of sequestered jury duty. MCA Records plans to open an office in Hong Kong to promote country music possibilities in Asian countries. Clearly, fans come in all varieties.

Country music performers are appreciated for their level-headed approach to life. As Hank Williams, Jr., says about his father, "No matter how many millions of records and how much money he made, he was living in the love of the common people, and he never forgot it. Not for one second."[33] Hank Williams, Jr. also points out that country music

> gave voice to people who had traditionally been ignored—even despised—the lower class southern white, the poor farmer, the wage earner, the workingman, the god-fearing family man, the bell hop, the black field worker. [It] was saying something they were hearing for the first time—that they were important enough to have somebody write the soundtrack to their lives.[34]

Ted Cramer, the program director for Kansas City's number one radio station, WDAF-61 Country, calls country music "three minute soap operas." Part of the appeal of country music, he explains, is that it is the most musical format. It is song-driven, with melodious but not complex music. It reflects the attitudes of many people. It doesn't require a special understanding or any kind of training to appreciate lyrically. And it is "every person's daily experience."[35]

Because country music is based on common, everyday events, if you've had any life experience, it can speak to you, unlike other formats that express unrealistic hopes and dreams or describe events and experiences outside the mainstream. Country music fans and performers alike can laugh at themselves. Self-deprecation is appreciated. People associated with country music cultivate this sort of attitude. Songwriter Whitey Shafer says, "Everytime I learn a new chord, I write a new song."[36] Though he has written many hit songs and is one of the most talented songwriters in the business, he feels obligated to present himself with a sense of humor. The country music classic, "You Never Even Called Me By My Name," makes a point of this. On the recording, the performer, David Allen Coe, tells a story about how the songwriter, Steve Goodman, said that this was the "perfect country and western song." But David Allan Coe points out that it isn't perfect because it doesn't say anything about prison, mama or getting drunk. So Goodman tacks on a perfectly silly verse including all of these things ("I was drunk the day my mom got out of prison" is just one gem of a line), and makes it a "perfect" (i.e., stereotypical) country and western song.

The country comedian also laughs at him or herself. Such comedians as Minnie Pearl, Grandpa Jones, and Jerry Clower are classic comics who are part of country music culture. Jeff Foxworthy, a more contemporary country comic, is appreciated for his "you might be a redneck" jokes. One example is "if you mow your lawn and you find a car, you just might be a redneck." His album, *You Might Be A Redneck If . . .*, reached platinum, the first comedy album to do so in ten years. The common incidents in life and in country music can be laughed at, but are never ridiculed and are always appreciated.

Country music performers, unlike, for instance, rock performers, make an all-out effort to meet their fans, do radio interviews, write columns for country music magazines, and even open their homes as museums. The fan base is active; grassroots popularity can make or break a country music performer. To cultivate this popularity, performers will go to a great deal of trouble. Garth Brooks, like other performers, is involved in the community. He takes time to read to elementary school students during "Read Me" day in Nashville. In Houston, country music is part of the curriculum at Tijerina Elementary School. Kids write to stars, fan clubs, and managers. Performers send gifts and information. Children research singers, write biographies, and use tour itineraries in geography class. When stars, like David Ball, pass through Houston, they often perform for students. Stars such as Alan Jackson, Suzy Bogguss, Eddie Rabbit, and others have participated. Students are allowed to go on field trips and participate in other activities but only if they have completed their other schoolwork. This motivational program helps keep at-risk children involved in their education.[37]

The public image of a country music performer is of great importance to both the performer and country music culture. As David Bryant, music programmer at WDAF 61-Country in Kansas City says, country music performers want to be perceived as "down home and grateful as hell."[38] To portray a country music image, one's act must be clean-cut (even if the performer wears his hair a little too long). Lewdness is never acceptable. Performers must appear above-board and likeable. This relates to the all-important sense of family; one can bring the kids to any country concert and not have to worry about what they see or hear.

The fans, of course, are integral to country music. Though many people regard truly devoted fans as passive, living vicariously through a favorite performer, country music fans are active in supporting and promoting country music, and in organizing activities, fairs and meetings. Numerous magazines and newsletters since the 1930s have provided an outlet for fan support and criticism.

The country music audience is considered older and more mature than the audience for other kinds of music, but many young people listen. Country music fans come from all walks of life, and advertisers try to target this diverse audience. In *Country Fever* magazine, the ads are from stars (thanking fans for their support), music clubs (twelve CDs for 1 cent), tourist areas, and contests.

In *Country America* magazine, which celebrates a country lifestyle as well as country music, one finds ads for food products, for Buicks, for detergent, and cigarettes, all aimed at women, much like the ads one might find in *Family Circle* or *Good House-keeping. Country Music* magazine can sport a jeans ad asking "tired of men only liking you for your brains?" Still, pickups and boots are also advertised, as are Nordic Track exercise machines, stereos, flea control, chewing tobacco. Western clothing, charitable appeals and cheap checks round out the advertisers.

Music City News, a slightly more sophisticated magazine, has ads for star merchandise, ads for guitars, guitar strings, guitar lessons, plus music workshops. A recent issue celebrated its 32 years of publication and many artists celebrated along with it, by taking out ads of support.

Randomly listening to country music radio reveals advertisements for a learning center, auto dealers, country music nightclubs, cellular phones, Clinique makeup, eye surgery and mineral water. Clearly, no single definition of the audience is correct. Traditional ideas of the country music fan are no longer true, if they ever were. Fans are just as likely to be bankers as farmers, lawyers as factory workers. Though the fan base is huge, and performers attempt to interact with their fans, still, the relationship between performer and fan is basically commercial. One can join a fan club to learn about one's favorite performer's life, and one is thereupon deluged with information on obtaining merchandise (not cheap, either). For $12 ($15 Canadian), one can join Loretta Lynn's fan club and receive a membership card and button, an 8 x 10 photo (color), a quarterly newsletter (and MORE!)

The Johnny Cash Fan Club, however, shows a more international flavor. For $13, one can join (US or Canada). Overseas costs $20. On my membership application, someone had pencilled in the words "Australia (23.00)," should someone from down under crave news of Johnny and June.

Garth Brooks deals with his fans in a novel way. He simply produces a magazine called *The Believer,* and dispenses with the fan club entirely. But as Valerie Clark suggests, if you are joining a fan club just for these advertised benefits (newsletter, photo, etc.), "you are missing the boat. These are simply rewards for your support," she says, "not things you should expect, or you will be disappointed."[39] The benefits of fan club membership can include preferred seating at the star's concerts, backstage passes, club events, newsletters and access to the performers' merchandise, as well as the feeling that one is part of something.

Fan clubs have been around since the late forties, though the idea of supporting one's favorite artist is probably timeless. Fan clubs continue to be successful even long after the performer dies or retires from the business. For instance, late stars such as Hank Williams, Sr. and Patsy Cline have very active fan clubs. Clubs exist for almost every star and for not so famous performers as well. As one writer points out, "unlike any other genre of music, country music has long been about the fans meeting their favorite artists."[40] Because country music culture demands much from a performer, those who don't measure up can be quickly abandoned, even though country music fans are usually very loyal. As fan club president Sherry Halton puts it, "there are some people whose personality is such that they don't like being around strangers."[41] Still, it is expected by most fans and performers that such interaction is part of the business—the country music business. "We're a little business," reports one fan club president, pointing out that this particular performer gets 5,000 pieces of mail each day. One employee opens the mail, others answer it, others fill shop-by-mail merchandise orders.

Sometimes fans get a little out of control—or are a bit crazy to start with, though actually very few fans ever threaten country music performers. Sometimes a country music performer is stalked but none have ever been seriously injured or killed, as was the case with the salsa star, Selena. The Robert Altman film, *Nashville* (1975) ended with the odd scene of a fan shooting a singer in front of the Parthenon. Still, for the most part, fans are polite and generous. Each artist attracts different kinds of fans. Most of the mail for the group Brooks and Dunn, for instance, comes from children eleven and under (which is ironic, since Brooks and Dunn have a Brooks and Dunn Visa credit card available to fans).

Country music has its share of respectable fans as well. American presidents including Jimmie Carter and Bill Clinton have admitted to their love of country music. As Clinton, an Arkansas native, says, "Where I was raised, we didn't know it was country; we thought it was the only music there was."[42] Other political figures have a closer relationship to country music. Former Louisiana governor Jimmie Davis is a member of the Country Music Hall of Fame. He was honored for his gospel recordings, most especially his signature song, "You Are My Sunshine."

Fans tend to be whole-hearted about their favorite performers. Their fans take them seriously, from the grandmother who has seen seventy-seven Ricky Van Shelton concerts to the fifteen-year-old who has just discovered Reba (country music, she says, isn't all that bad). One woman has seen one hundred and twelve Randy Travis shows; a different fifteen-year-old thinks Reba is a strong and caring person who is a good role-model.

Letters to the editors of various magazines try to articulate why fans are so loyal to their favorite singers. "I admire [them] for their personal values and priorities," says one fan, after pointing out that she could listen to their music for hours and never get tired of it.

Another fan writes, "I experienced a high risk pregnancy. The only real way I kept my sanity was by listening to country music on TNN and waiting for my issue of *Country America*. I think you should do a story on how country music helps heal and relieve stress or just helps people through tough times."[43]

One fan has a picture of the group Alabama tattooed on her arm. Another writes with chagrin that the "one big happy family atmosphere" is just a myth, because a well-deserving artist has been criticized by other performers. She then calls for a general boycott of the industry (except for her favorite artist).

Yet another reports stopping by Garth Brooks' house to take pictures. Brooks went out to meet her and asked if she wanted to take a picture with him. This fan included a photo to verify her claim, as do many of these letter writers.[44]

One writes "it has more meaning in my life than other types of music . . . It shares the feelings and dreams I hold inside that I can't tell anyone about and no one would understand." She comes from a tiny town and is grateful that country music performers continue to play in small towns.

Further, the Country Music Society Association newsletter carries personal ads from country music lovers who want to meet other country music lovers. Some happen to be incarcerated. Some are married people who just want penpals, but most are single adults interested in meeting other country music fans. They all list their favorite performers and often describe what country music means to them. One ad reads, "Lonely, recently widowed country woman needs country music fans to help her through."[45] An older couple is "willing to let younger and newer fans learn what we know."[46]

If performers are criticized in an article or in the "Letters" page of a country music magazine, loyal fans will write back, arguing about the criticism. Indeed, if an artist commits a faux pas, the incident is discussed with relish in these pages. An interesting dialogue ensues, though it requires considerable lag time between comments and responses. Letters express disapprobation. One writes, "I was disappointed to read about Mark Chesnutt. He had a lot of foul language in his interview. I don't like that. He could have used other words."[47] One writer says, "I was offended that someone who might seem to have some talent such as Shania Twain forgot to wear a bra in her video."[48] Some fans cancel magazine subscriptions when critics write negative reviews of favorite performers. Still, the majority of fans are interested in discussion, dialogue and negotiation. Country music appeals to them because it is about ordinary people and ordinary events. But the fans want to discuss the meaning of the performance of the music, the validity of any criticism; they interact with it just as lovers of literature interact with each other, and form their own fan clubs (that is, after all, exactly what the Dickens Society and the James Fenimore Cooper Society are).

One fan club president, Junior O'Quinn, who organized the Hank Williams, Sr. fan club, points out that country music draws fans because it tells a sincere story about life, a story that can relate to the fan in some way. As for Hank himself, O'Quinn says he appealed to people because he seemed to be singing directly to each individual listener.

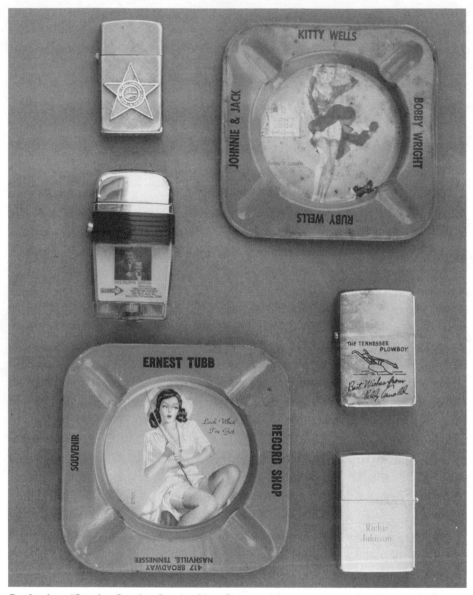

Back when "Smoke, Smoke, Smoke (that Cigarette)" was not considered as dangerous as Tex Williams sang, fans would treasure ashtrays and lighters featuring their favorite performers.

The annual weeklong Fan Fair, held at the Tennessee State Fairgrounds, is a sold-out festival of exhibits, events, concerts and times for the performers to meet their fans.

O'Quinn, who spearheaded the successful drive to put Hank, Sr. on a U.S. postage stamp, explains that the members of the fan club are from all occupations.[49] They are lawyers and bankers and even an American Ambassador to Mexico. Other country music performers such as Marty Stuart and Freddy Hart are members, as are people from all over the world, including England, Australia, the Bahamas, and Japan.

In addition to fan clubs, magazines, and so on, there are country music fan gatherings that allow fans to hear music, meet performers and get to know one another. The biggest of these is probably Fan Fair, the international country music fan festival held annually at the Tennessee State Fairgrounds. It was originally created in 1967 by the Johnson sisters (Loretta, Loudilla and Kay), who run Loretta Lynn's fan club. It isn't unusual for 25,000 people to show up, and pay $85 for admission to see forty or fifty performers. Fans listen to performers, then wait in line to meet them and get their autographs. Sometimes these lines are eight hours long. But the performers are also troopers; Reba, one year, signed autographs until four am the night of her fan club party. The west coast has Fan Fest, a slightly smaller version of the same thing. This gathering, held in Los Angeles each year, was started by the same group of people.

The loyalty of fans and the performer's willingness to put himself or herself out for the fans helps contribute to the appeal of country music. People tired of temperamental rock stars or unreliable urban rap singers can appreciate the qualities and character of these country music performers.

Country Music Influences

When country music performer Marty Stuart said, "I saw that country music and rock and roll were the same thing," he expressed the feeling common to many country music performers that the boundaries of folk, rock and country music are extremely porous.[50] The newly opened Rock and Roll Hall of Fame in Cleveland seconds this idea by including Hank Williams, Sr. and Johnny Cash in its list of inductees. Country music artists and fans insist that there is a country music sound, a sound that consists of a certain unity of theme and expression, but will admit that other musical forms have influenced country music. Rock and folk music have contributed instruments and amplification, for instance. Singers and songwriters have frequently "crossed over," achieving success with the same song on different charts, or appealing to two different audiences. Country music as well has had profound influences on other musical styles.

One of the first country music stars to crossover and find fans in a non-country audience was Patsy Cline, but other singers have proven important as well. They include Bob Dylan, Kenny Rogers, Emmylou Harris, and k.d. lang. These singers will be discussed and their songs examined by a process of short description, analysis of interesting features, interpretation and evaluation.

Patsy Cline

Hall of Famer Patsy Cline was the first important independent female singer in the country music tradition. Though her songs are often traditional chronicles of love and loss, her life was at defiance to traditional roles. Patsy Cline was born Virginia Patterson Hensley in 1932, in Winchester, Virginia. Her early years were marked by an abusive, perhaps incestuous relationship with her father who eventually deserted the family.[51] Her last performance was at Memorial Hall in Kansas City, Kansas, on March 3, 1963. Shortly after, she died in a plane crash.

Her brief career was important because she helped create the Nashville Sound, a smoother, more pop-like version of country music, which made it more palatable to a wider audience. She was also important because she opened doors for other women singers. She acted as Loretta Lynn's mentor and was never jealous of other women singers, though stereotypes at this time suggested that women singers could not work together. Loretta Lynn has called her a "woman's woman." She was regarded as a strong individual, intent on having her own way. Thus, as Barbara Mandrell points out,

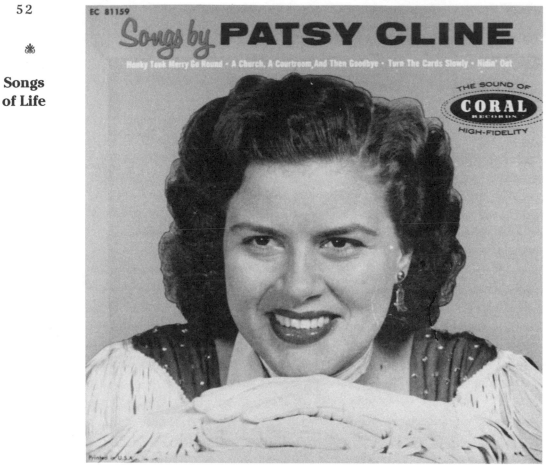

*An early and rare Coral Records album of songs by Patsy Cline. Coral was a Nashville
company organized to record country music.*

she was "just as in charge as any man."[52] Loretta Lynn, in her foreword to the biography, *Patsy,* writes, "Patsy didn't let nobody tell her what to do. She done what she felt
and if a man got in her way, she let 'em know they couldn't stand there. I thought that
was good of her. I think that's probably why I started writing like I did."[53]

Though Cline's music hit pop, rock and country charts, she wanted to be known as
a country music singer and resented attempts by various producers to make her sing
pop music. Originally she liked her hayseed image, and wore cowgirl clothes to symbolize her roots. Though she was represented as pert, bubbly and religious, she was
not. She said "too many hypocrites go to church," and she was actually a brash, heavy
drinker involved in numerous love affairs. She was not monogamous and her rela-

tionships were hardly traditional, though nonetheless she still sang traditional songs. She wanted to be identified as "country" because this linked her with a specific set of values that she wanted to represent. Her refusal to yield to other people's opinions was illustrated in the way that she championed Elvis—both his image and especially what he brought to country music—though other performers thought he was intent on destroying traditional country music.

Though she was an independent, unusual woman, she took time off in the late 1950s to become a mother (she had a girl and a boy). She created her dream home. By then, she wanted to be a middle class, respectable person, but eventually the stage lured her back.

This conflict followed her throughout her life. She suffered because of the disjuncture between real and ideal. The "Southern belle, . . . was the ideal: a woman of breeding, beautiful (but unattainable), talented (but not ambitious), and, above all, domestic. . . . Which put Patsy on a collision course with Southern Womanhood,"[54] says her biographer.

She appreciated her fans, developing friendships with them. "She was quite concerned with her fans," another performer says, "and not letting them down and them not putting her down."[55] Commemorated on a U. S. postage stamp in 1993, the biggest-selling artist MCA Records has ever had, her all too-brief-career opened doors for other women and let them say what needed to be said.

Crazy

In "Crazy," one of Patsy Cline's signature hits, the speaker tells herself that she is crazy for feeling the way she does—unhappy, lonely, blue. She knew her lover would not stay, that he would leave her for someone else sooner or later, and so she must be crazy for crying and even crazier for still loving him. The speaker is chastizing herself for feeling the way she does. This is a lyric song, one that captures a single emotion. In this case, the emotion is the singer's own self-disgust.

The song expresses single-minded pre-occupation with the speaker's state of mind. Though the emotion the speaker is focusing on is her feeling of despair, the song itself is more about the speaker's self-disgust than her despair. The lament suggests that while the situation is untenable, the speaker is unable to move forward. She has determined that she is crazy, but this is as far as her self-evaluation gets; she has no plans for curing her craziness or getting on with her life.

The speaker is clearly in great distress, wondering and worrying about her situation. While we observe that she is crazy—not in her right, rational mind—because she still loves someone who has hurt her, she is actually causing much of her own distress with her obsessive wondering and worrying about her feelings. She questions what she should do and what she should have done, and these questions also contribute to her state of mind. We sympathize with her while acknowledging her own participation in her "craziness."

The song succeeds in its clear goal—to convey a sense of the singer's despair. It was a great success for Patsy and helped create a wider audience for country music.

I Fall To Pieces

"I Fall To Pieces" recounts the problems the speaker has whenever her former lover walks by. He wants her to pretend they have had no past together, that they are just friends, but she can't do this. Every time he is near, even if she's with someone new, she falls to pieces. She's incredulous that he wants her to behave differently, and she is also amazed at her own inability to maintain her composure. This is another lyric song, capturing the sense of embarrassment and frustration the speaker feels.

The speaker is clearly embarrassed and frustrated that her former lover still causes her to fall to pieces, in particular since he has made it plain that he no longer cares. The lament is repeated over and over—the former lover comes near and the speaker falls to pieces. Yet, we are prompted to ask why this seemingly inescapable cycle is repeated. What causes her to keep seeing her former lover? Is it deliberate on her part? One can speculate that she walks by her old lover while in the company of a new lover for the express purpose of making the former lover jealous. However, this purpose fails and the speaker is left in pieces.

The speaker is caught in a situation painfully familiar to most adults. The repetition of the chorus ensures the feeling of being trapped and unable to escape from the situation. Meeting her lover over and over, whether the act is accidental or deliberate, evokes the frustration and impotence the speaker feels at being unable to control her emotions. Further, the speaker points out that time doesn't help. The time-honored cliché is that time will heal all wounds and yet she insists that time only adds to her pain, increasing her wound. Clearly, the raw hurt of unrequited love is at work here, but it is exacerbated, perhaps, by the speaker's expectations in conflict with the former lover's expectations. He wants to be able to ignore her and he doesn't want to be embarrassed by her emotional response. He doesn't want to be responsible. Yet her expectation, since she meets her former lover over and over again, is that something positive will come of these meetings. Yet it never does. With the passage of time, it becomes less likely that his response will change, less likely that he will return to her and less likely that she will learn not to care. It is this awareness that causes time to add to her pain. As time passes, and he remains out of reach, she fails to heal and most likely never will.

This song expresses a common country music belief or motif—that is, not only is failure in love painful, but one can do nothing about the pain. One is personally unable to control one's emotions. This fairly typical country music motif was again exposed to a wider audience as "I Fall To Pieces" became an important hit for Cline.

She's Got You

"She's Got You" is another lyric song that captures a feeling instead of describing a series of events. The speaker lists the "things," the objects she has been given by her lover: a picture, records, his class ring. She points out that they remain the same—the picture is still signed "with love," the records still play the same songs, and the class ring is still a token of his love. Only one thing has changed; the speaker has these things, but another woman has the lover who gave them. The speaker says that all she has now are these memories, and then she asks "or have they got me?" She relates her emotional situation in a bemused but despairing way.

Again, the wronged woman is in stasis; the memories do indeed have her, preventing her from moving. Such songs capture the moment of pain, but do not promise any further solace. In "She's Got You" it is clear that these little things have no value to the man, for he hasn't asked for them back, but the speaker has invested them with volumes of meaning. They are, and have been, significant to her, and she is overwhelmed that they no longer mean anything to her lover. A sense of jealousy is apparent in the speaker's reference to "she," but the speaker's familiarity with "she" is as much owing to the speaker's ongoing examination of the situation as anything else.

The word "got" places the lover in the same category as the material possessions he has left with her. The speaker has "got" the picture, the records, and the class ring, while another woman has "got" the lover, almost as if he had no volition of his own. It is as if the song is about these two women and their various possessions, and not about the man at all. The speaker does not express animosity towards the other woman. There is no suggestion that the man was wrongfully stolen or that he can or should be "got" back. The speaker is merely relating her feeling of unreality. Everything is the same, except this one thing, and its absence changes everything. Though the speaker insists that the objects have not changed—the picture is indeed still signed "with love"—it is apparent that they have. Their meaning has been radically altered, for they have meaning in relation to the man, who is no longer involved in the speaker's life. The objects seem the same, perhaps just as the man seemed the same before he left, but the objects are different, as is he, since he is in the possession of a new love. The objects now only represent memories, and these memories have the speaker trapped.

This much loved, very successful song cemented Cline's appeal to a non-country audience while at the same time it shared a relevant country music message and revealed Cline's mature vocals.

"You Belong To Me" is a bit different from the songs just discussed. The speaker's lover is leaving on a trip and she reminds him that as he sees the pyramids, the jungle, the ocean, he must remember her. She knows she'll feel lonely and she is afraid he'll be lonely, too. The speaker must content herself with reminding the man that "you belong to me."

Here, the speaker feels threatened not by a specific woman, but by an event. Her lover is temporarily leaving, but she fears the separation might become permanent. It is loneliness that is the danger here—his loneliness. The speaker fears that he will fall victim to that all-to-human tendency to seek comfort wherever it is available. Her admonition—you belong to me—doesn't seem to be sufficient incentive to keep him from straying, so coupled with the loneliness she anticipates feeling, she will have concern that he will find someone new or might simply lose interest in her, especially when he might meet fascinating and exotic others.

The speaker must remind her lover over and over again that he belongs to her. She seems to be reacting to his eagerness to be gone. The "Grand Tour" he will be taking echoes the Grand Tours that young men of means have historically taken before returning home to settle down. She anticipates his return, for presumably he will settle down with her, but she dreads the thought that it might change him. The man's Grand Tour might actually be a tour of duty in the military service, since that was an experience for almost all young men in this time period, and while the speaker doesn't express any fear that he will be hurt, she is well aware of other potential hazards. As she details the sights he will see, she constantly reminds him of her, so that he might think of her when he sees these sights. We are under the impression that all her efforts will prove futile.

Like other country music songs, this one deals with the fear of losing a lover. The song was not as successful as other Cline hits, but again, the imagery, vocals and country music sound all appealed to a wide audience.

Patsy Cline's contributions to country music are immeasurable. Not only did she lead the way for other female artists to succeed in the country music industry, she appealed to a wide variety of fans, including those who did not usually listen to country music.

Bob Dylan

In the late 1960s, a branch of country music called country rock developed from the folk and rock influences prevalent at the time. The folk influence on country rock can be heard in its politically and socially-aware lyrics. Bob Dylan's music is often considered country rock, even though he wouldn't meet the criteria set by some tradition-alists. His influence on other country singers, however, was great.

As anti-Vietnam war attitudes developed, Bob Dylan emerged as an important songwriter/narrator. Songwriters, of course, always describe the human condition, but as Charles T. Brown says, "Country music is one of the most conscious expres-sions" of this,[56] and Bob Dylan eventually concurred.

Dylan recorded both *Nashville Skyline* and *Blonde on Blonde* in Nashville during the late sixties, and his association with Johnny Cash influenced both of them. Before 1969, when *Nashville Skyline* was recorded, Dylan's reputation had been based on such songs as "Blowin' in the Wind," other protest songs, and signature ballads such as "John Wesley Harding." The *Nashville Skyline* album represented a new Bob Dylan, singing country songs with plain country lyrics with the Nashville Sound in the back-ground. Advance orders were so strong that the record company applied for Gold Record Certification even before the album had been shipped to record stores.[57]

During this period, Dylan appeared on Cash's television show. He remarked in an interview, "these are the types of songs that I always felt like writing when I've been alone to do so. . . . I admire the spirit of the music."[58]

In an interview about his friendship with Dylan, Cash said, "They say they can't un-derstand how we could be friends. Some people I like, some people I don't like. He can sing and he feels what he sings. That's all there is to it. I regard him as a friend of mine because of that."[59]

Born in 1941 in Duluth, Minnesota, as Robert Zimmerman, he was declared the spokesman for his generation when he was only twenty-one, since his songs ex-pressed important messages about his generation's political and emotional lives. As one critic pointed out, "A nationwide audience clung to every word, based major life decisions on single lyrics, built prophecies on every song."[60] This was an unusual ac-colade for a singer-composer born Jewish on Minnesota's Iron Range.

In 1966, a motorcycle accident forced Dylan out of the spotlight and into seclusion to heal. Not until 1974 did he perform in another concert. His albums grew more or less happy and content until a bitter, messy, and very public divorce took place. Re-cently, Dylan has become a born-again Christian, prompting Joan Baez to say his songs with Christian messages "are horrible music."[61] In 1993, he sang with and wrote songs for Willie Nelson's *Across the Border Line*. He is still involved to some extent with country music and his influence on a new generation of singers is immeasurable. Per-formers such as Mary Chapin Carpenter, Suzy Bogguss and Rosanne Cash have named him as a musical influence.

When asked what his songs are about, Dylan once replied, "I do know what my songs are about. Some are about four minutes; some are about five, and some, believe it or not, are about eleven or twelve."[62]

Bowden, in her critique of his performances, says, "neither he nor his audience . . . ever meant to limit a song to that one [recorded] performance as somehow the correct one."[63] As an example, she cites the song "It Ain't Me Babe." In six performances, it meant six different things: "variously a happy love song, a statement of political protest, a shout of triumph, a ritualistic commonplace, an escapist reassurance, and a devil-may-care denial of responsibility for her hurt."[64] Therefore, it is not always possible to separate the performance from the song.

She also points out that without words, his music—melodies and chord changes—like most country music, would be boring. For Dylan, as for others, the message is the thing. She also says, "Although Dylan's songwriting and performing style have developed . . . the subject of most of his songs—like most all songs ever—is love."[65] In his *Nashville Skyline* album, many songs tackle the more sophisticated themes of country music.

Girl From The North Country

In "Girl From the North Country," a duet with Johnny Cash, the speaker addresses a person who might be going to the fair. If so, the speaker asks that he be remembered to a girl who lives there. The speaker wants to be certain the girl is taken care of. He asks to know if she looks the same way he remembers and he wonders if she is thinking of him.

One of the most enduring questions country music tackles is "does my former lover ever think of me the way I think of him or her?" This song addresses that subject. The speaker would like to know that his former lover is just as he left her—and he would also like someone to remind her of his existence, should she have forgotten. The idleness of this interest is apparent in the fact that the speaker has no intention of pursuing her himself; perhaps he is warning the other away from her, but the point remains that he himself doesn't plan to do anything to answer his own questions.

The speaker is indulging in some nostalgia, looking back at the past but he is also interested in the relationship of the past to the present. The answer to the question—is she the same?—is not necessary because he still cares about her. It is necessary for his carefully constructed memory of the past. The answer will also help him with the meaning of his present life. Is he the same as well? How has he changed? The song resonates with links to the folk song, "Scarborough Fair," which details a similar situation. Here we see how the past defines the present.

Of the songs on the album, this is the most "folk." Since it was sung as a duet with Johnny Cash, it shows the relationship of folk and country music and demonstrates the influence each style has had on the other.

In "Lay, Lady, Lay," the speaker invites a woman to stay the night in his "big brass bed." The speaker recounts his longing for her and is frustrated by her (apparent) lack of interest in him. He describes how he wants to see her in the morning light, implying a willingness to commit to more than just a one-night stand.

The speaker allows all of his private feelings to be revealed in this raw, emotional lyric song. He expresses his desire for a woman whom he calls lady. He seems a bit in awe of her; whether she is actually from a higher social class or is merely pretending, we do not know. It is possible the speaker is being polite, for his barely restrained passion for her causes him to attempt different approaches. He tries to convince the woman that he is worth the time and that his intentions are honest and genuine.

The speaker asks her to stay in "my" bed and then, referring to himself, says, "his hands are dirty." He speaks of himself in both the first person and the third person. The speaker makes his personal address, his personal appeal (stay with me) but then seems to remove himself to escape her rejection. But this "objectivity" also allows him to see himself as she sees him: his clothes are dirty, but his hands are clean. These two features are highly symbolic. His dirty clothes suggests a blue-collar status, a rough-and-tumble existence that casts an unmistakeable contrast to the "lady." Whatever her background, it is clear a working class man is not her ideal. Yet the speaker insists that his hands are clean, which indicates not only that his heart is in the right place, but that he is honest and authentic. Only wrongdoers and dishonest men have dirty hands, he implies. He seems to be trying to convince her, and himself, that he is worth any number of rich city boys.

"Lay, Lady, Lay" has been covered by other artists, notably Eric Clapton. Its appearance on a country music album and its subsequent appearances on rock albums shows the ability of country sound songs to cross music boundaries. Many people who know the Eric Clapton version are surprised to discover its original source, but the song is in the tradition of country music.

Tell Me That It Isn't True

"Tell Me That It Isn't True" details the speaker's anxiety about his relationship. He has heard rumors that his lover is going to leave. These rumors say that she has been seeing someone else. He counts on her to say it isn't true, and only asks for her to say so. This lyric song captures the uncertainty of the speaker—he is afraid he is losing his lover, but he does not want to admit it.

Though fearful of losing his lover, the speaker is powerless to do anything about it. For this reason, he doesn't want to hear the truth. He never even asks for the truth. What he wants is for her to say the rumors are not true, regardless of whether they are

❀

**Country
Music
Influences**

or not. We can sympathize with him; he would prefer not to know what he knows. The closest he can come to that former state of innocence (of not knowing) is by requesting her to deny the charges. Still, we know, as does the speaker, that he can't recover that state of innocence no matter what his lover tells him.

The speaker puts the proposition to his lover in simple and straightforward terms: tell me you aren't cheating on me and I will believe you. The speaker can be seen as desperate. So unwilling is he to lose his lover that he simply refuses to face the possibility. Yet another interpretation is possible—defiance. Yes, she has been seen around town with a tall, dark and handsome man, but the speaker doesn't care. He simply wants to be able to say that she has said the rumors are not true, which will allow him to keep his pride. In fact, some of the lines can seem almost menacing as he tells her that she had better come through for him, as if the greater threat to their relationship would be her unwillingness to lie.

The song, though not one of the most popular songs on the album, nonetheless details a common-enough situation, but handles the theme with subtlety and authenticity. Infidelity and its consequences have always been of interest to country music, even when other musical styles shied away from addressing the issue.

Tonight I'll Be Staying Here With You

In "Tonight I'll Be Staying Here With You," the speaker throws his train ticket, his suitcase and his troubles out the door, because tonight he will be staying with his lover. He says he should have left, but he can't. She seems to have cast a spell. So, the speaker concludes, if there's a poor boy leaving town, he can have the seat, because "tonight I'll be staying here with you."

The idea of the lover who is going to leave but is drawn back and stays with his lover is a rarer but by no means unknown love song theme. Here, while it is apparent that the speaker has abandoned his idea of leaving, he has only abandoned it for tonight. His staying is only temporary, not permanent, so his original decision to leave still stands and has merely been postponed, which is not necessarily a satisfying solution.

Though the speaker makes no permanent change or commitment, the song manages to capture the joy that can occur when one acts in a spontaneous manner, and seizes the moment, as it were. Country music commonly suggests that love and happiness are only transitory, temporary aberrations in a rather treacherous and often despairing existence. This song celebrates, as do others, these temporary moments of happiness. If only we can learn to appreciate such moments, these songs suggest, the rest can be endured.

With this song, Dylan comes almost full circle. Though not all of the songs in *Nashville Skyline* are touched on here, Dylan writes on almost every common love theme in country music, and this song is no exception. The audience he reached was different from the country music audience, and so he made the music appealing to non-country listeners.

The importance of Bob Dylan to country music is apparent, not only because he made the music available to a new audience. He was a model for other country music artists, in particular the newer stars who cite him as a musical influence. But country music also had an influence on him, not simply because he sang these country songs, but also because the opportunity to compose and sing country music influenced his later compositions as well.

Kenny Rogers

Kenny Rogers is another important crossover artist. Though he has some songs that do not deal with love (for example, "Reuben James"), most of his repertory as a country music artist is about love relationships.

Born in Houston in 1937, he was the fourth of eight children in a very poor family. His first gained fame with a rock group called The First Edition; the popularity of this group began to wane in the early 1970s. He went solo in 1975, but did not do well at first. However, in 1977, his song "Lucille" went to the top of country and pop music charts. His crossover success was due to his pop-like voice and musical arrangements. He also capitalized by singing duets with other well-known performers, such as Dolly Parton, which helped to legitimize his career and to increase his popularity. As a country music singer, his importance is due to his enormous success as the first real crossover artist. His songs have consistently been successful on both popular and country music charts, and he has been constantly in the media, in movies, on television and in concert performances.

Though some criticize his music as bland, popular music, he is a sound musician who appreciates and is appreciated by his fans. For many years after that first hit in 1977, his success was assured. By 1989, however, he was beginning to decline in popularity and could not guarantee a sell-out crowd. One reviewer felt that Rogers had moved past the point of conviction with his material, and once that happens, fans can tell—and will stay away. Though Rogers was and is warm and likeable and continues to interact with his audience with the same self-deprecating charm of the most popular country music stars, he seems to have moved away from country music. He hoped the song "Planet Texas" would return him to the graces of his fans, but it proved to be too odd and unlike Rogers and country music to appeal to his usual audience. "This can be a whole new career move," he said at the time, though it did not prove to be so. Still, Kenny is known on a first name basis around the world, just like Aretha and Elvis, which is some comfort to him. He still manages to excite the tabloids, whose headlines say: "Kenny Rogers Shock! His Son To Wed Porn Star." Still very much in the media, he has become more of a personality than a performer.

By 1995, he was honored by having a cerebral palsy center named after him for his fundraising efforts. Rogers, the recipient of the 1990 Horatio Alger award for achieving success from an impoverished beginning, doesn't expect to always be successful as a country music star and has put his energy into other activities. His Kenny Rogers Roasters fast food chain projected openings of stores in Greenwich, Connecticut, and Fresno, California, plus Nicosia, Cyprus, Kirion and Beer-Shava in Israel, Tokyo, Korea, Malaysia and the more prosaic El Paso and Memphis. Other ventures include the Showboat Branson Belle, which offers dining and entertainment and is modelled after the old Mississippi river steamboats.

Though Rogers has covered a number of songs by other artists— "But You Know I Love You," which was made famous by Dolly Parton, and "Today I Started Loving You Again," which was made famous by Merle Haggard, he is known however for a number of songs that are his, like "The Gambler" to which he brings his distinctively gravelly voice. His most recent album was a collection of romantic songs from the 1930s and 1940s—not exactly the country music sound.

Ruby, Don't Take Your Love To Town

In "Ruby, Don't Take Your Love To Town," the speaker is a man wounded in a crazy Asian war. He pleads with his wife not to take her love to town, though he can no longer satisfy her. He would like to shoot her, but his own condition—which has caused her behavior—thwarts him.

Like most of Rogers' songs, this ballad tells a story of two people; his story-like narratives require little interpretation and indeed leave little room for interpretation. One simply enjoys listening to them as to a good story. The speaker in this song, however, is not actually addressing his wife, for he is watching her preparations from some distance away. When he hears the front door close, he shifts from ostensibly addressing her to deliberately addressing us, the audience. When he makes his empty threat of shooting her, his reference is to "her" not "you," a difference that means he has abandoned the pretense of talking to her. We realize he is talking about her and that he is asking us to vindicate his emotions; he is asking us to be on his side.

The song, while a straightforward account of a man's frustration, also plays against the tension inherent in the mention of a "crazy Asian war." The speaker says he was happy to fight as he was supposed to, but it is clear that he was not expecting the sacrifice he would make. The anger and bitterness here are a result of the war, but are directed to a personal, domestic sphere. As is often the case with country music, global issues are addressed in regard to their effects on personal lives, allowing the results of political or social policy decisions to be made apparent and realistic to the audience.

As a showcase for his story-telling voice, this song does exactly what it is supposed to do. While very much a song in the country music tradition, Rogers' approach and voice allow non-country fans to appreciate the sentiments as well.

Reuben James

"Reuben James" recounts the story of a black sharecropper who is blamed for all the troubles in a small town, but who is the only person willing to take in a young orphan. The speaker (the orphan) tells of Reuben's many kindnesses and how he taught the speaker right from wrong. The speaker mourns Reuben's death.

This is a love song of another kind—a son singing a loving tribute to his "father." The song also serves to reveal the hypocrisy and cruelty of allegedly good and moral people who are willing to abandon an infant merely because its mother engaged in loose behavior. Reuben, who teaches the speaker to turn his other cheek, is the one person who doesn't turn his back on the child. Further, we can see that Reuben's kindness is repaid, though he never expected it to be. He simply did what was right and good.

The subtext of the song deals with racial tensions. The only person blind to race in the song is the black sharecropper. The others are not only racist, but they are morally inferior in other ways as well, being willing to abandon a helpless orphan, as they are interested only in appearances and social status.

This song, one of Rogers' hits, puts a slightly different twist on the standard tribute song, emphasizing, as it does, love and kindness as ties that bind, rather than blood and family.

Lucille

"Lucille," too, is a simple story. The speaker, a man in a bar, is approached by a woman who is looking for fun and happiness. The speaker is interested and is making arrangements when the woman's husband walks in. The speaker's first fear is that he'll land in a fist fight, but this is a false alarm. The husband merely asks the woman how she could leave him at this time, the worst of all possible times. She has not only left him, but four children as well—and "a crop in the field." The husband makes his statement and leaves, but the speaker's sympathy obviously lies with him, for after the confrontation, he cannot feel the same way about the woman. This becomes apparent as they attempt to continue what they have started.

Clearly, the speaker is examining his own motives and responsibilities. The woman seeking a casual affair, and willing to leave her husband and children for it, is merely a reflection of the speaker and his obviously skewed values. It is not his fault the woman left her husband, but he feels as if it is. Not only that, he feels her failure to meet her obligations has turned her into an unattractive individual.

A simple narrative, the song details how the speaker's emotions move from desire for a woman to sympathy for her husband and, finally, to distaste for the woman's behavior. As he runs the gamut of emotions, we empathize. But another tension is at work, not merely the tension of infidelity. The conflict between country life, which the woman's husband represents, and city life, which the speaker represents, is also an issue here. Country life, as evidenced by the hardworking farmer-husband is good and honest, but it can also be boring and dreary, his erring wife feels. The free and glamorous city life is symbolized by the man at the bar (the speaker) who seeks a casual affair. But that life can be tawdry and empty, as he realizes after the farmer has confronted the woman.

"Lucille," of course, is the song that thrust Rogers into the spotlight and allowed him to go on to stardom. The song is important as well for it captures the conflict of country versus city life. While Rogers is to some extent symbolic of the city (he is considered sophisticated and urbane), his understanding of the country ethos as shown in this song made him seem authentic and acceptable to his fans.

Daytime Friends

"Daytime Friends" describes a woman whose husband is cheating on her. For comfort, she calls her husband's best friend. The two may be lovers by night, but during the day they must pretend they are only friends. They both have too much to lose. They do not want to lose what they have, but they need each other as well. They themselves are hurt, yet they fear hurting others. The situation is never resolved and remains ambiguous.

The song differs slightly from other Rogers' songs. It recounts a story—the wife's husband calls to say he is working late, so she calls the best friend, and so on, but the story itself is secondary to and is overshadowed by the emotions generated by the affair. The conflict that is set up is the focus of the song. The phone calls that are recounted are only some of many; they symbolize something that has gone on for some time and will continue to do so. For this reason, there is no real beginning, middle or end. The affair is not driven by spite. It is initiated for comfort and because a mutual attraction exists, but the relationship is complicated by guilt and subterfuge.

The ambiguous and unresolved ending reinforces the nature of what they are doing. Neither plans to take any action, either to further the affair or to end it. Their stasis is a sort of living punishment for what they are doing. They see no way out that doesn't entail further pain. The feeling of being caught in a vicious circle of one's own making is admirably captured here.

The song captures a sense of the affair as being punishment enough, for neither the speaker nor the singer condemns the affair. It merely is. Like other country music songs that deal with infidelity, this one refuses to glamorize it, but also refuses to apologize for it. Infidelity simply is, though it causes great pain. This song, a popular crossover song, shows that concerns with the realities of love and love relationships are important to non-country music fans as well.

Rogers has concentrated on singing ballads which describe a situation or event. He relies on narrative and on his storytelling ability to attract his audience and deliver his message. His best-loved songs are those that follow these general guidelines.

Emmylou Harris

Emmylou Harris was born in Alabama in 1947. Growing up in the South, she was nonetheless drawn to folk music at first; she cites Bob Dylan as an important influence. Like several other country music singers, including Mary Chapin Carpenter and Suzy Bogguss, she wasn't raised on country music but discovered it. "My friends and I had grown up on rock and still loved rock, but we also fell in love with the poetry that was country music."[66]

By the mid 1970s, she had become popular—but as a country music performer. Her duets with Don Williams are distinctly country and while she experiments with folk and blues, she remains country. Her importance stems from the way she "united old-line country conservatives and rock-loving liberals in a common cause and a common sound. She gave country music back its pride in its heritage."[67] Since she appealed to several different audiences, she helped expose many listeners to country music.

A middle-class fan who enjoyed country music throughout her childhood, she started her musical career in the coffeehouse folk scene, a venue noted for its interest in political and social issues. "I do best when I have a crusade,"[68] she says. She has been a staple of the country music scene for twenty years and more.

As songwriter Pam Tillis remarked, "In high school, if you wanted to be a pop singer, you wanted to be Joni Mitchell. But if you wanted to be a country singer, you wanted to be Emmylou Harris. There are artists who set the standards that everybody else follows."[69]

Though Harris has been singing for years and has influenced an entire younger generation of country music performers, she has only been a Grand Ole Opry member since 1991. In June of 1995, she joined other country music artists in releasing a gospel album, *Amazing Grace: A Country Salute to Gospel.* She is a former president of the Country Music Foundation; she now serves as a vice president.

Her stage presence is often compared to that of Kitty Wells and Loretta Lynn. She has received several Grammys and has produced many albums, each of which has sold at least 500,000 copies. She has won awards for her work with Dolly Parton and

Linda Ronstadt as *Trio*. Her songs appear almost exclusively on country music charts, though her music also appeals to fans of folk, rock and pop. These days, her new, more acoustic and less electric stage show appeals to those who also admire Mary Chapin Carpenter.

She points out that "especially in country music, the real good songs tend to have a universal appeal. How could you ever outgrow a Hank Williams song? It just shoots for the bullseye."[70] In 1992, Harris recorded the 140-year-old song, "Hard Times Come Again No More," written by Stephen Foster. "I see songs in an unbroken procession. No matter when they were written, if they hold up lyrically, I see them as fair game."[71]

One critic says, "most of the country music world is in awe of Emmylou Harris."[72] Though she opened doors for people like Garth Brooks and the Judds, she has not benefitted from the commercial boom of country music in the 1990s. Programmers consider her old guard. Since she lacks airplay, it has been ten years since she has had a Top 10 country music album.

Harris says it is the words that interest her in music. Though sometimes a songwriter, she feels her job is to find and interpret songs. "I think it's good not to give yourself a lot of time to think about things," she says, "Follow your instincts, what feels right. Artists should never think."[73]

One Of These Days

"One of These Days" describes the speaker's vow that things will change—"one of these days." She says she might be a woman dressed in black, she might be gone with the wind, she might go across country singing (as loud as she can), and whatever she does, she won't have to keep everything bottled up inside. She will have peace of mind.

While other songs recount the speaker's vow that she will leave soon, with the implication that she won't, this song suggests that the speaker is considering a whole new way of life. If she is willing to make the big change by leaving, she can or might make these other changes as well. She is considering what persona she could adopt, who she could be if she left. The images she chooses are unusual and interesting, reflecting carefully thought out choices, not merely generic or happy images. Still, she has not decided on when this metamorphosis will take place, only that it will be "one of these days." As we know, "one of these days" often never comes.

The speaker equates leaving with self-expression. Not only will she be able to say what she thinks and not have to bite her tongue for fear of alienating someone or hurting someone's feelings, but she will also be able to express herself in other ways. She says she could dress in black; in a country music culture, this conjures up images of Johnny Cash and what he stands for. She can do the same thing. This expression of self is clearly stifled in the love relationship she has. We can judge, then, the nature of the relationship even without having to learn any details about it (which we don't).

Obviously, the speaker is unhappy, because otherwise the speaker would not consider leaving. We can easily imagine the lover ridiculing the speaker's ideas of what her new life will be like.

This song showcases Harris' beautiful, smooth vocals, though she is clearly singing country music, as she mentions the wayward wind and the troubles on her back, using characteristic guitar twang and fiddle picking. The song is also one of many of her songs that celebrate the ability of women to get along without men. Others include "To Daddy," and "Easy From Now On." This attitude is not one that has always been expressed by country music performers and makes it a refreshing, while still authentic, message.

Making Believe

"Making Believe" concerns a woman who is unable to recover from a broken relationship. The speaker is alone and blue, but she pretends that her former lover still loves her. She knows she will never have him, she will never hold him close, and so making believe is all she can do. The lover has met someone new, and so the speaker knows he will never be hers. She laments that her plans for the future will never come true, but instead of making new plans, she will spend the rest of her life loving him and making believe.

Here, the speaker has been so hurt by her lover's desertion that she has retreated to a child's game of make believe. She is obviously unable to cope in an adult manner, for even her stasis and her inability to recover have a child-like basis—she plans to simply pretend the break-up never happened, and she will make believe they are still together.

The desire to retreat from adult cares and hurts is one expressed by many artists and while the speaker here insists that there is nothing else she can do, she is simply choosing this course, and we can sympathize.

This song follows a country music tradition of inability to move beyond a failed love relationship, very much in the tradition established by Patsy Cline (many of whose songs Harris has covered) and Hank Williams. This song updates that tradition (it was written in 1976) for a new generation of country music fans. Again, Harris' smooth vocals and crossover influence allowed many folk and pop fans to listen to country music.

Two More Bottles Of Wine

"Two More Bottles of Wine" tells how the speaker and her lover hitchhiked out west and found a place to live. Two months later, he moved out. He just up and left. But she's not going to worry about it, because she has been working hard and is tired. She points out that she is almost two thousand miles from anyone she knows, she is sleeping in a warehouse in west L.A., and she is doing all she can to make it, but opportunity rarely shows up. But she doesn't resent what has happened or her situation, because, as she also points out, she's tired, it's midnight and she has two more bottles of wine. We can bet she plans to drink those two bottles of wine to drown her sorrows.

The song is much more narrative in form than Harris' other songs. It tells a story and details how the speaker plans to deal with her current situation. Though, as she points out, she is abandoned, barely able to make a living and thousands of miles from her home, she is not completely despairing. She doesn't have time. The song is about facing difficulties with clear and realistic resolve.

The song alludes to the country music motif of drinking to ease the pain. But what is being celebrated here is the ability to deal with difficulties and uncertainties. The speaker is hopeful, not despairing, though she is realistic about her situation and her frustrations. The song shows the transitory nature of love and love relationships. What started out as a happy, exciting adventure has gone sour and the speaker has found herself with a completely unexpected change in fortune. However, she plans to deal with this bad luck with hard work and determination.

This is one of Harris' most famous songs, and probably one most responsible for her crossover success. While the song details a painful situation, it has a strong beat and sounds uptempo, a bit of a departure for Harris.

Boulder to Birmingham

In "Boulder to Birmingham," written by Emmylou Harris, the speaker says she doesn't want to listen to a love song or hear a sad story, presumably because she feels sad enough as it is. The last time she felt like this, she says, she was in the wilderness. She says she would walk from "Boulder to Birmingham" if she could only see "his" face again. Like other love songs that suggest what the lover would do for love, she makes her promise. But she knows she will not be asked to perform the feat. This lyric song captures an emotion of longing.

The imagery the speaker uses suggests that she is lonely, perhaps afraid, and very much isolated. The song gives few details of the situation the speaker is in. In fact, the "he" she refers to could be anyone: a lover, a father, a civil rights leader.

The lack of guidance makes this song open to many different possibilities. The goal is to evoke a feeling of solitude and can be applied to many situations. The references to burning fires and Abraham suggest a lament about civil rights, but the reference to a man who "really got me this time" suggests a more personal pain and abandonment. The ocean, mountains, and wilderness all make appearances, symbolizing various states of mind.

This song is one of only a handful that Emmylou Harris has written. It is, of the songs she has recorded, the closest to folk music. It works to expand the sound of country music a bit beyond its usual boundaries.

Emmylou Harris has been an important figure in country music, a legendary performer who is still active and still works to perfect her sound and her message. Since she has always appealed to pop and folk fans, she has helped to bring the country music sound to other listeners.

k. d. lang

k. d. lang, the first openly lesbian country music performer, poses a big problem for country music. People like her music, but not her country "punk" image. She is called the non-conformist of country and has received little radio airplay. She's simply a little too odd to be accepted completely by Nashville. Still, her albums have sold well and she has a loyal concert following. In addition, she is respected by other country music performers, including Loretta Lynn, Kitty Wells and Brenda Lee, all of whom appeared on her recording, *Shadowland*.

k. d. lang (she prefers the lowercase spelling of her name) was born in Consort, Alberta, Canada in 1961, two years before Patsy Cline died, though later lang would say she was the reincarnation of that singer. lang did not grow up a country music fan—she was in college before she became interested in it. Her band, the reclines, were named as a pun on her feeling that she is Patsy reincarnated, or at least has a spiritual connection with Cline.

Her stage show is lively, energetic and eccentric. Its pace is frenetic, marked by ad libs and physical punctuation to the music. "Elvis is alive and he's had a sex change," says one reporter.[74] Her approach changed ideas about what female country music performers should and could do. She writes much of her own music, some of it humorous ("Watch Your Step Polka"), but she covers many musical genres. She was, in fact, playing at the Edmonton Folk Festival when her first country music song came out.

Her kind of country music attracted listeners who were not accustomed to listening to country music. Still, this, plus some of her public stands, have alienated her traditional country music audience. Her intelligent, ironic performance of country music seems to some as if she were making fun of country music, which fans do not appreciate.

But lang has the freedom that many country music performers would like to have. Seymour Stein, the founder of Sire Records, states her contributions in his oft-quoted remark, "You are what country music would have been if Nashville hadn't screwed it up."[75]

Her critical acclaim has been great. She is so well regarded by some insiders that she was able to bring the legendary Owen Bradley, Patsy Cline's producer, out of retirement to work with her. Her critical acclaim included a Grammy in 1988 for a duet with Roy Orbison of "Crying," her best known song. She was also named, in 1989, Best Female Vocalist (in a tie with Tracy Chapman) by the *Rolling Stone* magazine critics' poll. Another Grammy came in 1992, when she was voted Best Country Music Female Vocalist.

She calls country "white North American blues," touching on the fact that it is an ethnic music, one that leaves many minorities cold. lang says she appreciates the country music culture and tradition but wants to revive its sense of humor. For this reason, she says, "country music was way overdue to have an androgynous singer."[76] She has answered critics of her appearance by saying "it would be detrimental for me to compromise. . . . The country industry is traditional regarding the looks and roles of men and women."[77]

Her audience consists mostly of women; lang lets her fans express themselves freely. She is adored for her goofy antics, passionate delivery and bizarre wardrobe. She wears combat boots, not cowboy boots. She wears oversized men's shirts, in contrast to other female country music performers, who stick to cowgirl dresses or evening gowns, or perhaps jeans and tailored shirts. The singer has broken country music barriers and has acquired a following in the rock world. She has reached many new fans—people who don't ordinarily listen to country music. But her presence confuses many country music fans. Does she love country music or is she contemptuous of it? People who find progressive country appealing—as it is expressed by performers such as Lyle Lovett and Dwight Yoakum—often appreciate her, while traditional fans do not. She says of country music, "I had an empathy for and understanding of the country perspective, of the openness that country teaches you."[78]

The critics have raved about her intelligent, philosophical music, though mostly she sings love songs. She made a major career mistake when she taped a promotional spot for People for the Ethical Treatment of Animals, one of the most radical of the animal rights' groups. She said "meat stinks," and "if you know how meat was made, you'd probably lose your lunch." This angered people in cattle country. Dozens of stations dropped her from their playlists. Many listeners called in to say that they didn't want to hear her music. The overwhelming feeling was one of betrayal. Her fans had supported her, but she did not in turn support them. She is aware of her estrangement, and though she is identified as progressive country and is the recipient of awards for country music, she has never been nominated for a Country Music Association award. She has also received criticism for blasting the male-oriented and male dominated country music industry which makes it harder, emotionally and professionally, for women to succeed—as artist, producer, or promoter.

Western Stars

lang's song, "Western Stars" is in the tradition of Hank Williams, Sr.'s "I'm So Lonesome I Could Cry." In "Western Stars," the speaker is alone and lonesome. The stars keep on shining, though she is apart from her lover, and she is convinced her heart will break. The wind blows, and she is alone and crying.

This most traditional of songs attempts to capture and record a single emotion. Again, natural objects like the wind and the stars are invested with the speaker's emotion and carry the imagery.

Like other country music songs that do not detail a complete story or provide minute descriptions of the speaker's life, this song captures an emotion but leaves the understanding up to our imaginations. The speaker has been left by a lover and she feels alone; the stars are a symbol of that aloneness, isolated as they hang in the sky, but beyond this, we can interpret the meaning as we choose.

As a song in the tradition of Hank Williams, this admirably carries on the lyricism of his music.

Black Coffee

"Black Coffee," an old Peggy Lee standard, is a bit of a play on all those drinking songs for which country music is justly famed. The speaker is feeling lonely. She is thinking about her lover, who has done her wrong. She makes some fine generalizations about the nature of men and women and drowns her sorrows in black coffee and cigarettes instead of the requisite whiskey or beer.

Still, the image of the speaker drinking black coffee and smoking cigarettes evokes the emotion it is intended to evoke, without using old clichés. Drowning one's sorrows is a time-honored pastime, but this song gives it a new twist.

The song gives us a new way of looking at a common country music situation. While often a person drowns his or her sorrows in alcohol, in this case, the speaker is drowning her sorrows in black coffee. But we realize the destructiveness, which we have always assigned to the alcohol, is actually inherent in the situation. It is the need to drown or eliminate one's feelings that is the problem, not necessarily the route taken to do so.

This song received a fair amount of airplay on country music radio stations, allowing country music fans to become familiar with lang, as other audiences had. As a drinking song that puts a twist on what is being drunk, it was appreciated by fans who enjoy hearing new perspectives on old motifs.

Shadowland

In "Shadowland," the speaker says that since her lover has gone, she lives in shadowland. She laments her dreams that now are shadows, too. She asks why her lover had to go and wonders what mistake she made. Then she protests that she is not a shadow, she is a woman who loves and her lover should come and lead her out of shadowland.

This lyric song evokes the image of a person being reduced to a shadow, losing substance and density. The speaker recognizes that while she feels different (a shadow of her former self) she really is not different. This acknowledgment is important, for she recognizes that she should not and cannot stay in shadowland. But again, the speaker is impotent. She cannot imagine devising or finding a way out of shadowland but can only call on her former lover to return and lead her away. Since he abandoned her there in the first place, it is difficult to imagine him returning to lead her away. Because of her impotence, she is likely to stay in shadowland forever.

One can only imagine what shadowland is like, but presumably it is frightening. Indeed, though the speaker describes her feelings of loneliness, fear must be present as well. In such a place, it must be difficult to accurately judge anything. All clarity and wisdom would be lost. It would be difficult, if not impossible, to determine what was real and what was illusion in such a place.

This is the title cut from lang's most country album, and is a brilliant, though eerie, evocation of darkness, despair and hopelessness. Though less well-known than other lang songs, it still captures a country music lament in the tradition of Hank Williams, and lang's inspiration, Patsy Cline.

I'm Down To My Last Cigarette

In "I'm Down to My Last Cigarette," the speaker is waiting by the phone because her lover said he would call. She describes how late it is—her coffee is cold, other people are in bed sleeping. Any reasonable person knows he won't call this late, but she's waiting and now she's down to her last cigarette. She knows if she runs to the store, he will call while she is out of the room. But if she doesn't get more cigarettes, she will go crazy with the waiting.

The song is a brilliant rendering of how the feeling of pleasant anticipation (he'll call soon) turns to concern (he may not call) and then to despair (he didn't call, so I must be a bad person.) Almost every adult woman can identify with this song, in particular the frustration and exasperation tinged with self-doubt and unhappiness.

The song is a straightforward description of a common situation. The speaker feels various emotions, but instead of blaming the lover who hasn't called, she is unwilling to admit that he won't call. To admit that would mean that other feelings and fears would have to be acknowledged and the speaker isn't quite ready for that yet. The song actually validates a common frustration women have and by recognizing it, allows women to identify with the speaker and the singer as well.

This, too, is among lang's songs that received country music radio airplay. It appealed to a number of female fans in both country and other genres because it captured a common occurrence and the feelings connected with that situation.

lang is important as an influence, because her traditional country music style found fans among non-country music listeners. Further, lang challenged many traditional and cherished assumptions in the country music industry. Her unusual wardrobe, outspoken behavior and sexual orientation all served to shake up the country music culture and forced it to reassess its values and beliefs.

❦

All of these artists have influenced country music. Some have attracted audience members who wouldn't ordinarily listen to country music. Some have added non-country elements to their music. Still others have spread country music through crossover success. Each of these singers has dealt with the themes and messages of country music, regardless of their own original musical orientation, and has helped country music expand its horizons. By the same token, they have helped spread the word about country music, showing that it can appeal to people of all varieties, classes and situations. Country music continues to grow and change as it absorbs material from other musical styles and it continues to exert its influence on other musical genres as well.

Past Issues

In contemporary country music, major thematic issues concern love, living, women's roles and social or political concerns. Of these, only the discussion of women's roles, introduced in the late sixties and early seventies, is new. The other themes have existed from the beginning. The British folk ballads that inspired country music focused on these three concerns—love, living and social/political concerns. While country music has added new perspectives to these issues, the issues themselves are timeless.

In the past, however, other issues of importance surfaced—prison, traveling, cowboy life. These were not and are not daily experiences, but were still highly symbolic and highly evocative themes. Such themes concern isolation from others and disconnection from the larger community. These issues are symbolized by word portraits of prison, wandering, cowboy life, and so on. While such images are present in contemporary country music, and the underlying concerns are still present, the songs construct their meanings much differently. Songs about prison and about wandering have given way to songs that tackle issues of isolation and aloneness in different ways. Songs that deal with prisons and trains, however, while they may not be produced very often today expressed a country music ethos and still inform the music of today. Further, some earlier singers capture issues of love and living in a slightly different way than contemporary singers do.

Some of the performers who best capture these past issues are Ernest Tubb, Kris Kristofferson, and Merle Haggard.

Ernest Tubb

Ernest Tubb was one of the founding fathers of country music, and his influence continues long after his death. Not only do his songs influence younger stars, but throughout his life, he formed many mentoring relationships with younger singers.

Tubb was born in 1914, in Crisp, Texas, outside of Dallas. His mother was his earliest musical influence and from his youngest childhood, he admired Jimmie Rodgers, whose style he imitated early in his career. Rodgers' widow arranged for Tubb's first recording session and was instrumental in helping him launch his career. She identified the same sincerity and feeling in his voice that her late husband had always considered most important in a singer. Tubb always took his singing seriously, though it

Poster for appearances of Grand Ole Opry stars Ernest Tubb and Hank Thompson, in Des Moines, 1963.

was many years before he was taken seriously. He insisted that his music be referred to as "country," not "hillbilly," a shift that increased the stature of country music.

In 1947, at the first country music show ever to be held at Carnegie Hall, Tubb headlined. By then, he was the acknowledged master. He influenced another honky tonk singer, Hank Williams, and sang "Beyond the Sunset" at Williams' funeral. Tubb, along with Hank Williams, was considered a pioneer of the honky tonk style of country music that drew millions of fans to country music in the 40s and 50s. He recorded more than 800 songs, wrote more than 150, and sold 30 million records. The "Texas Troubadour" was called one of the "Four Pillars" of the Grand Ole Opry, the other three being Bill Monroe, Hank Snow and Roy Acuff.

Tubb was renowned for his kindness in helping others get started and stay on top during rough periods. His kindness and endurance have given him his nicknames — "The Great White Father of Country Music" and "The Satchel Paige of Country."

He was an active musician until his death. Even late in his career (and life) he was making more than 200 appearances annually. After his first appearance on the Grand Ole Opry, he received 3,000 pieces of mail—and it never stopped. A member of the Grand Ole Opry since 1943, he continued performing there for almost forty years, until 1982. His audience appreciated him because he always said that he wasn't doing anything the next "ole boy" couldn't do as well. Tubb's fans were at ease with him. His nephew says that people were just as happy to hear him talk as to hear him sing. Tubb always had time for his fans, and his male fans probably outnumber his female fans, an unusual situation in country music.[79] One music executive described his popularity this way: "I was with him for many years in Texas where people would hear a Tubb song and think they were listening to the National Anthem."[80]

Ernest Tubb was elected to the Hall of Fame in 1965, almost 20 years before his death. Individuals are selected and voted on by an anonymous group of two hundred participants. Each member of the Hall of Fame has been involved in country music for at least fifteen years and is deemed to have contributed significantly to the industry. The elections are sponsored by the Country Music Foundation, which owns and operates the Hall of Fame. Only a few dozen people have been elected to join this distinguished group.

When Tubb first appeared in concerts, his fans were poor, rural and could relate to his music. Typical of the 40s style of country music, he was able to appeal to country music fans, but the music did not have a mass appeal until late in his career. Country music did not cut across class lines at that time, though Tubb worked hard to make it appeal to a larger group.

During the Second World War, the shortage of materials prevented manufacturers from pressing as many records as fans demanded. After the war, when country music fans still had difficulty getting country music records, Ernest created an all-country music record shop. The Ernest Tubb Record Shop, around the corner from the old Grand Ole Opry building in Nashville, houses the largest collection of country music recordings in the world. This spurred other retailers to add country music racks, thus increasing exposure for country music artists. About a year after the shop opened in 1947, Tubb came up with the idea for the Ernest Tubb Midnight Jamboree, a musical event that ran, and still runs, for an hour after the Grand Ole Opry broadcast ended. People still stop by to listen to the musicians perform at the Midnight Jamboree, which helped launch stars such as Johnny Cash, Patsy Cline, and Elvis Presley.

In the 1940s, Tubb began his movie career, a very important venue for him as for most of the country music performers of the day. While he played a variety of roles, he always found the opportunity to sing. Though poorly scripted and poorly acted, the movies presented the music—which was the point.

Tubb's last years drew admiring fans from "divergent social, political and economic levels, and under an ever-increasing variety of guises . . . It is a bewildering, yet somehow greatly reaffirming, sight to see the Okie from Muskogee standing alongside the hippie from Mississippi . . . while Ernest laments over honky-tonk angels or lost letters, or lonely soldiers."[81] Tubb explained, "The kids today are looking for down to earth realism" and country music provides that.[82] All he asked was that they keep their long hair clean.

Thus it was that many people mourned his death on September 6, 1984; he was 70 years old and had battled emphysema for some years.

Thirty Days

Tubb performed a variety of songs that celebrate a certain country music ethos of losing, of leaving, of being away from home. Yet these themes are presented with a certain amount of clear-eyed objectivity. One song in particular that illustrates Tubb's sense of irony is "Thirty Days." Here, the speaker's lover has left and he gives her an ultimatum. She has thirty days to come back home. Of course, he has no leverage at all, nothing to entice her with or force her back. All he can offer are comic threats. He's going to get a warrant from a judge and have the sheriff arrest her; if that doesn't work, he's going to the FBI, and if that doesn't work, he is going to the United Nations. His threats seem more ludicrous as his anxiety and desperation increase.

But the song makes one smile; this is merely a man who is smarting from the hurt to his pride and is making idle, empty and even harmless threats. His inability to attract her back is his flaw, but we don't feel that the figure is tragic or even very sad. No one seems to be particularly heartbroken, but we can ruefully identify with his hurt pride.

The song falls somewhere between a ballad and a lyric. It tells something of a story—but it's not much of a story. It tells something of a feeling—but it is not much of a feeling. What the song captures is Tubb's detached assessment of the speaker. We can hear how ridiculous the speaker sounds as he makes his blustery threats. But, we slowly come to realize, the speaker is equally aware of how ridiculous his threats sound. He is only making them because he has to save face somehow. He knows, as do we, that what he is doing is unsuccessful.

One of Tubb's better-known songs, this one allows the listener to appreciate the sophisticated use of irony and detached objectivity that Tubb brings to his music. It helps to show that even some of the earliest country music was intelligent and thought-provoking.

Thanks A Lot

In "Thanks A Lot," the speaker says he's got a broken heart and that's all—"thanks a lot." He hears that his former lover is not sorry about leaving him and thinks he deserves it, to which he replies, "thanks a lot." He remembers how they loved a little and laughed a lot and again says sarcastically, "thanks a lot."

The tone here is sarcastic rather than ironic, but nonetheless, something has been lost. Again, we have a sense of the speaker's inability to do anything about the situation, except respond sarcastically to its different elements. Instead of revealing in detail all his pain and sorrow, he sticks to a simple "thanks a lot," which speaks volumes.

This song again focuses on a failed love relationship and the speaker's chagrin at that failure, which he evidently did not anticipate. The speaker here has a different assessment of the relationship than his former lover has. He clearly misunderstood her, for he is surprised at the things she says about him. However, instead of being hurt and angry, he settles for merely making a sarcastic remark or two. Obviously, his pain and anger would mean nothing to her, and might even please her, and so he refuses to give her that pleasure.

Another of Tubb's best-known songs, this is one that treats failure at a love relationship in a sarcastic, almost off-hand manner. Clearly, the speaker is hurt by the desertion of his lover, but instead of responding with a tear-drenched sonnet, he vents a little spleen in this honest account.

Pass The Booze

In "Pass the Booze," the speaker is very lonely, even though he has friends with him. He says there is only one way he will sleep tonight, though it is clear he doesn't mean sleeping so much as passing out. He tells the bartender to take his address down in case he forgets it, and describes his plan to sit at the bar and drink until his memory of "her" is gone.

In this song, certain traditional elements of country music lyrics come to the forefront. Like other songs which emphasize drinking, this one makes it clear that sometimes one must drown one's sorrows in alcohol. Country music is often criticized for the number of songs which seem to celebrate drinking, though these songs are probably an accurate reflection of how people actually do attempt to deal with difficulty and pain in their lives.

While the song can be seen to simply depict a person who plans to drink to forgetfulness, drinking in country music often represents something beyond the mere physical act of drinking and getting drunk. The motif is best understood if the idea of drinking is actually taken to represent an interior emotional distress. Drinking is symbolic of emotional rupture and distress; the drinking merely acts as an outward sign of this interior conflict. If we examine this song—and others like it—on a more metaphorical level, we can see that it deals with an individual in such distress that no other people can help him or her. The only cure, temporary as it may be, is to become completely numb. The permanent cure would be death, but people in country music songs don't choose this. Drinking to insensibility, then, is merely an imperfect imitation of death, an attempt to become numb to feeling.

Again, as one of the early popular country music songs, this song is one of the original "drinking to forget" songs which are and have been such a staple for country music. As a typical example, it shows the traditional elements of a country music drinking song. Since singers now have an increased awareness of the dangers of alcoholism, many contemporary drinking songs are written from a much different perspective.

Walking the Floor Over You

"Walking the Floor Over You" details the speaker's actions after his lover has left. He is pacing the floor, he can't sleep and his heart is breaking. He describes how his lover left and said she would be back, but she lied. All he can do is hope that someday she'll be lonely, too. He advises her if that is the case, then she should walk the floor.

Here, the speaker is thwarted. Not only was he betrayed and taken by surprise—she never confronted him—but he was never able to vent any feelings about the situation. All he can do then is hope, with petty vengefulness, that she'll be in the same situation some day. But although he has been through it all himself, he will not be able to feel sympathetic—only derisive. Walk the floor, he counsels her, it's good for you.

Again, the speaker recounts a situation where he has failed to sustain a love relationship. He has been deserted, but as in other Tubb songs, we are not sure why he has been abandoned. It isn't necessarily because his lover found someone new. That excuse is often used in love songs, but Tubb rarely buys into it, showing instead that relationships fail because of internal reasons, not external ones. This means his speakers do not have the luxury of being able to blame someone else for their own failures. In this song, the speaker is obviously hurt and angry—he is pacing the floor—but again, instead of explaining the details of the abandonment and subsequent pain, he prefers to dwell on what he hopes will happen to her some day. His bitterness is clear, but even his revenge is passive. He does not intend to do or say anything hurtful to her, until she has been hurt herself and finds herself in a similar situation. Then he will gloat.

This popular Tubb song offers an alternative to tear-soaked sonnets about failed love relationships. Taken together, these songs indicate, to some extent, the detached view and sophisticated irony possible in country music, a detachment and irony indicating an intelligence not notable in other styles of music in this era.

Tubb's use of traditional themes of country music and his position as a well-regarded, highly influential performer affected the country music business for dozens of years. His music still informs the styles of many of the current generation of singers.

Kris Kristofferson

Kris Kristofferson is among the most intelligent and talented people to sing country music. Born in Brownsville, Texas, in 1937, he became interested in literature in college and earned a Rhodes Scholarship for study at Oxford. He served in the Army Rangers, graduated from Army paratrooper school and served in Vietnam. In 1965, he decided to try to make it in Nashville as a songwriter.

Kristofferson had two children from an early first marriage. In 1973, he married singer Rita Coolidge, with whom he made several records; they had one child before their divorce in 1980. After a period of battling alcoholism, Kristofferson married Lisa Meyers and has had several children with her. Kristofferson's image slowly evolved from a young man in a neat suit and tie to a bearded, rugged individualist in a t-shirt and jeans. Though his background is a bit unusual, he is actually a very mainstream country music writer and singer.

He catches the country music ethos of love, Sunday morning hangovers and other facts of life. In the 1970s, however, he began to act in movies and has become less involved with country music. His involvement in films marks a change for country music artists. While he may sing on the soundtrack to a film, or showcase a song or two during the course of a movie, he was never hired because of his singing ability. It was his popularity as a singer that made him an attractive prospect as an actor. His personality and his image were the qualities producers were seeking. His films have included *Alice Doesn't Live Here Anymore* (1974), *A Star is Born* (1976), and the notorious *Heaven's Gate* (1980). A number of television movies and appearances have kept him busy throughout the 1980s and 1990s.

Kristofferson was able to connect with people who had not related to country music before. He, of all country music songwriters, is the one most usually regarded

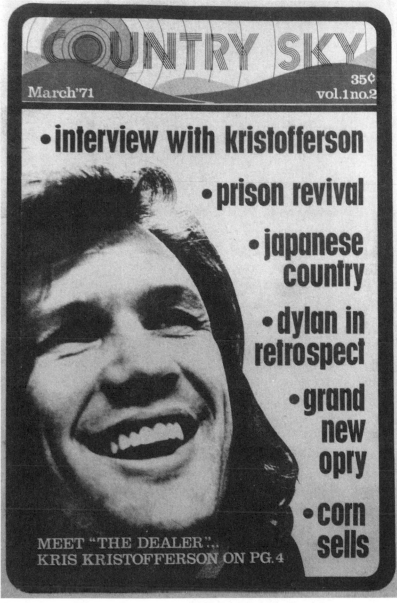

By 1971 Kris Kristofferson, featured on the cover of Country Sky, *was winning success as a songwriter and as a performer of his own material.*

as a poet, with his gift for recreating moments, dialogue and emotions exactly. His music is very close to the folk ballads, country music's original source material. Some of his music laments being alone, some prizes freedom. His most famous country music hit as a singer is probably "Why Me?" This personal, religious song was an almost immediate hit. Kristofferson says that when he first began writing songs, the melody would come first and then he would put lyrics to it. But country music taught him to start with the lyrics and then add the other elements.

As a member of the group The Highwaymen, he now tours with Johnny Cash, Willie Nelson and Waylon Jennings. One critic has called this group "country music's Rat Pack," and has said that it consists of "the four corners of a living legend skyscraper." The music these four men produce has been called "outlaw zen."[83] Kristofferson manages to evoke clear and sharp images while dealing with themes common to country music. He deals with losing, drinking and personal salvation in ways that differ from contemporary country music singers.

Me And Bobby McGee

"Me and Bobby McGee" is a song of loss. Two lovers drive across country and become intimate. The speaker is able to share his secrets with her. She is warm and supportive, a good companion. But somehow, he lets her slip away. She was looking for a home, which he presumably could not give her. He hopes she'll find that home.

This song, also covered by Janis Joplin, has the famous line, "freedom's just another word for nothing left to lose," which became a tag line for an entire generation. The speaker again has allowed something easy and worthwhile to get away from him. Still, his regret is not that she's gone, but that he couldn't supply her with what she needed. That is, he knows that she could return but he still would be unable to settle down. It could not work; since it was inevitable, in a sense, though it is much lamented, the speaker feels it was impossible to prevent.

In this song, the lover laments a lost love, but knows he could have done nothing to prevent it, since he could not offer his lover what she needed. Nonetheless, the speaker's need for freedom is shown to be a hollow, worthless desire—freedom just means one has nothing left, which is a perspective the speaker had to learn through such losses.

This song of a failed relationship, like Tubb's songs, is one in which the speaker accepts responsibility for the loss. As a song that easily crossed over to the pop and folk charts, it showed the permeable nature of such artificial music boundaries.

Help Me Make It Through The Night

In "Help Me Make it Through the Night" the speaker invites a woman to sleep with him. He tells her all he is doing is simply taking up some of her time. He claims that it doesn't matter what is wrong or what is right, all he knows is that he needs someone, a friend, tonight. He is not concerned with how he—or indeed she—will feel tomorrow; his need is too pressing right now. He is lonely and alone and wants to fix that somehow.

In many ways, this song functions like a drinking song; the only way to exist with such emotional devastation is to find some way to numb emotions; instead of drinking, the speaker thinks another person will distract him. Of course, he is counting on a sexual encounter with a stranger to numb his emotions, which it very well may, but that does not make it a very attractive offer for either of them. He assumes that his emotions won't be engaged by the other person, and so he might be able to escape from his feelings. Such a sexual experience could help the speaker handle distraught emotions; the little death that results could mimic the numbing effects of alcohol— imperfect but better than nothing.

This raw appeal can be compared to Bob Dylan's "Lay, Lady, Lay." But here the woman is not wanted for herself, but for the comfort she represents. It is clear that any woman would do, and it is rather easy to imagine the speaker making this appeal to several different women before finding a willing one. That a woman might be willing to take the speaker up on his offer suggests that he is targeting someone who is as devastated and needy as he, which certainly does not bode well for future happiness. But that is not the point. The point is to survive the tortures of the night, however that can best be achieved, and deal with the horrors of the morning on the morrow.

As a rather explicit depiction of a brief sexual encounter, the song, rather than offending the country music culture (which is considered socially conservative) actually acted on country music listeners' own sense of empathy and allowed them to connect with the emotions instead of judging the morality of the situation. In the tradition of country music songs bluntly tackling divorce and infidelity, this one addresses sexual promiscuity.

Sunday Mornin' Comin' Down

"Sunday Mornin' Comin' Down" details the morning after a drinking binge, when, sober, the speaker takes stock of his life and doesn't like what he sees. His head hurts no matter how he holds it. He has only dirty shirts to wear. He sits outside, smoking and watching children play. He wishes he was drunk again because he feels alone. All the events serve to reinforce his loneliness and isolation; he doesn't belong in a normal, everyday Sunday school world and he recognizes this. If he were drunk, he would be in his element and could cope.

The dreary cycle is clearly established. The self-disgust he feels at his drunkenness can only be alleviated by his drinking; by drinking, he isolates himself and alienates others. When he is sober he is lonely, isolated and alone, which makes him want to drink. No song better captures the despair of an alcoholic unable to change his life.

Like the drinking song, the effects-of-drinking song is a time-honored tradition in which the condition of the alcoholic is described. In this case, the alcoholic understands that his condition is not glamorous or exciting or even fun, but he is nonetheless incapable of making a change or even accepting that a change is possible. In this way, the drinking man is the wanderer, the traveler, because he is isolated and exiled from the community. While drinking is not celebrated here, there is a suggestion that the purity of being alone is almost worth the pain of isolation. Although the song doesn't glamorize or celebrate drunkenness, it serves to show the individual's complete individuality, untouched by others. That pure individuality is somehow both cause and effect of the alcoholism, and drinking is a natural by-product of the loner's natural need to be alone. Since individualism and even the tortured individual are revered in country music, the self-destruction in evidence here seems natural and inevitable, with no possibility of change.

As an effects-of-drinking song, this clearly captures the unhappy cycle of the alcoholic. At the same time, it presents a view of alcoholism as an inevitable result of a tortured person's life and so excuses the problem. The song moves away from the simple drinking songs and examines what uncritical use of drinking as a method of forgetting can do to an individual.

Why Me?

"Why Me?" is a personal, religious song. The speaker asks God, "Why me?" Why did God give him all the blessings He did? The speaker knows he hasn't done anything to deserve such blessings and wants to know why they have been given. The speaker realizes he has ignored or wasted much of God's love and he commends his soul to Jesus. He says he will try to repay it all by trying to show others the love of God.

This song is typical of country music theology; the humble singer is not worthy of God's love but gets it anyway, which is a miracle worth rejoicing over. Because it so clearly embraces the typical religious message, it became extremely popular.

The song gains meaning in relation to other songs in Kristofferson's canon. As a singer who details the moments of tortured living familiar to all, Kristofferson is seen as a speaker for those who have been down, broken, in pain. In general, his songs are about finding solace—although of a temporary nature—in sex and alcohol. Here, the speaker finds solace in a personal, spiritual sense; this solace is more permanent in nature.

This is Kristofferson's most successful and most famous song. It deals with spiritual salvation, one of the basic concerns of country music. It is probably the most famous non-gospel religious song ever recorded, appealing to a wide variety of people, of a wide variety of creeds.

Kris Kristofferson's songs deal with issues that preoccupied country music in the past. In particular, his songs describe individuals who must attempt to alleviate pain through drinking and other self-destructive activities. His most important song, however, was one embracing a spiritual connection to God, sung in the religious tradition of country music.

Merle Haggard

Merle Haggard is best known for his "Okie from Muskogee" and "Fighting Side of Me" songs about the Vietnam war, which are considered very conservative and anti-liberal. President Richard Nixon even sent Haggard a letter praising the song "Okie," which Nixon asked Johnny Cash to sing at a White House performance. (Cash refused.) Though best-known (perhaps notorious) for this song, Haggard's style, lyrics and career have grown and developed since the 1970s. His songs, nonetheless, focus on those themes that were emphasized in the past—prison, travel, and so on.

Haggard was born in an abandoned railroad car in 1937 in Bakersfield, California. His father was a fiddler who passed on the country music tradition to him. Haggard was in trouble during his youth and ended up in San Quentin prison in 1957; Cash played there while Haggard was an inmate.

In the early 1960s, Haggard began working as a musician in Bakersfield. His first huge success was "(My Friends are Gonna Be) Strangers" in 1965. His early tunes were sentimental and traditional like "Okie," but he began to embrace a broader vision. "Make it Through December," for instance, is a mature song with a political connection. "Big City" is similar. His themes deal with home, prison and personal self-searching. Like Cash, who sings about prison and performs for prison inmates, Haggard also sings about such experiences. Even now, the prison experience is a pertinent one to country music. In 1995, for example, Marshall Chapman recorded a live album in a women's prison. Still, the mystique and glamor associated with prison and prison images is no longer accepted by country music culture.

The son of a migrant worker from Oklahoma, Haggard has won more than 30 major music awards since 1965. Almost forty of his songs have reached number one on the country music charts. He was elected to the Hall of Fame in 1994. Often called the poet of the common man, he expresses the hopes, dreams and fears of blue collar Americans. A legendary performer, he appeals to many younger adults these days. As one critic points out, he is among those country music performers who are "so vocally unique that if you hear them sing two words you recognize them."[84]

Mama Tried

"Mama Tried" is one of those songs that celebrate Mama, trains and prison, which all seem appropriate to Haggard's life. The speaker says the first thing he remembers about life is the sound of a train. The speaker, when he is old enough, leaves home on that train. He says his mother tried to stop him, but he wouldn't listen. The speaker

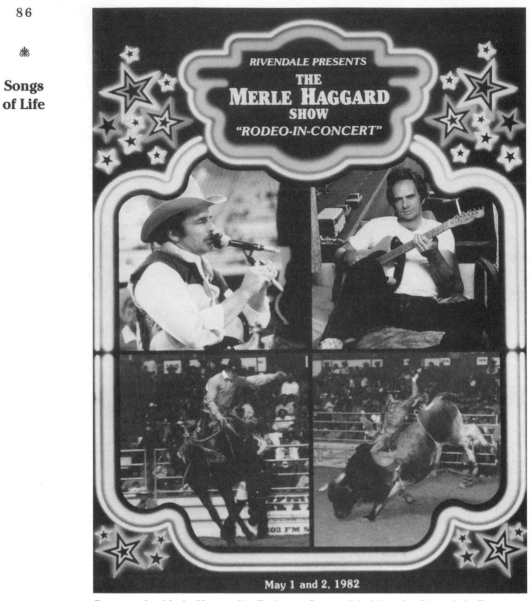

Program for Merle Haggard's "Rodeo-in-Concert" held at the Rivendale Entertainment Center, Valencia, California, 1982.

tells us that he "turned 21 in prison doing life without parole," one of the most famous lines in country music. He reminds us that his mother tried to raise him right, but he rejected her teachings and so can only blame himself because "Mama tried."

The song is interesting because although the speaker accepts full responsibility

for his past actions, this responsibility does not help him avoid a future life of crime.
There is something unsatisfying about an individual who says he is at fault but never
tried to stop. So for all that it might seem to celebrate the prisoner, the song does actually condemn him.

The speaker here details the events of his criminal life, and the events certainly
seem believable, as if they might really have occurred, but the images evoked are
nonetheless highly symbolic. The train whistle he remembers as the first thing he ever
heard, the sound that set the tone for his life, so to speak, we immediately recognize
as a symbol of freedom—in particular, freedom from constraint and boundaries. This
makes his ultimate incarceration both believable and sympathetic. Indeed, "Mama"
herself is highly symbolic, too, standing for all that is loving and decent and worthy.
When he rejects her, these are the qualities he rejects as well. The speaker's subsequent actions and imprisonment are only to be expected after he has rejected all that
is loving and decent and worthy.

This is one of Haggard's best known songs, and it captures the very essence of
these themes that once preoccupied country music—prison, trains and Mama. It is
significant that one major reason for the popularity of this song is the sense fans have
of its authenticity. That is, they believe such events could have been and actually were
lived by Haggard.

Okie From Muskogee

"Okie From Muskogee" is probably Haggard's most famous song. He says that in
Muskogee, people don't do drugs, they don't burn draft cards, or have long hair; they
fly the flag proudly and the kids respect the college dean. Even squares can have fun
in a place like Muskogee.

While the song represents a very conservative point of view, with a speaker who is
proud of Muskogee, it is supposed to be a wry and ironic commentary on the nature
of these conservative people in this small town who are unthinkingly jingoistic. The
way the song was embraced by conservatives and rejected by liberals, each of whom
took the message literally, overshadows its actual point. Haggard himself thinks it is
the most misunderstood song in country music and expresses amazement and embarrassment at the reception that greeted the song. Haggard expected people would
at least recognize the tongue in cheek quality of the song, but they did not.

As has been demonstrated by the audience response to this song, on occasion a
song can mean one thing to the singer/songwriter and another thing to the listeners.
In this case, a more sophisticated meaning was intended, while fans and detractors
alike settled for the simple, most readily apparent meaning.

The song was extremely important as it represented a position that a certain segment of the population held during the Vietnam war. In fact, it could be considered the

anthem of the conservative crowd. Regardless of Haggard's intentions, the song developed a life of its own and became an extremely popular pro-war song.

I'm A Lonesome Fugitive

"I'm A Lonesome Fugitive" records the speaker's feelings while he is on the run. He says that he behaved wrongly when he was younger. The speaker laments the fact that if he stops running, he will spend the rest of his life in jail. He must stay alone, so that he can travel faster, though he would like to settle down.

Through the use of certain metaphors, the speaker communicates a message which has a very "country" feel to it. The speaker says when he was younger, he sowed his wild oats and his mother prayed the crops would fail. The cliché serves as a bit of folk wisdom, while allusion to crops reminds one of the country background at the heart of the song. The speaker evokes the image of prison, though this prisoner is not in jail, as well as the image of traveling.

The fugitive is often seen in a romantic light, especially, as in this case, when the fugitive regrets whatever crime has caused him to be pursued. The tragedy of his life is admired and marveled at—though the wanderer is celebrated, it is also recognized as a very unsettled, essentially unhappy, way of life. The fugitive's change of life and character make him a redeemed sinner, also dear to the heart of country music culture, but his past has condemned him. The interaction of past and present (the one defining the other) is of interest for though very much situated in the present, country music does look to the past to find meaning and direction.

The song admirably expresses the past issue of traveling—in this case combining the threat of prison with forced exile from the community which makes this very isolated figure the focus of sympathy, but also romanticizes him. The loner—the outlaw in particular—resonates with meaning today, but was especially important in the past.

(My Friends Are Gonna Be) Strangers

"Strangers" describes the snowball effect of betrayal. The speaker says he thought that he and his lover would be together forever, but it turned out to be a short forever. He turned his back once and she was gone. He says that he isn't going to trust anyone from now on—even his friends are going to be strangers to him. He expresses surprise at his own naïveté and gullibility. It occurs to him that he was foolish for trusting her— or anyone—in the first place, and he vows never to do so again.

The song expresses how anger and bitterness in one aspect of life can spill over and affect other areas as well. When the lover leaves, we might understand the situation of desertion. Or, since he indicates that he turned his back once, there might have been some greater failure on his part, enough to drive his lover away. Nonetheless, her betrayal has further repercussions.

At its core, this song is about a failed love relationship. Since the speaker's lover has deserted him, he feels bitterness and pain. Yet, since he can't punish her in any way for her desertion, he turns instead to punishing his friends. He has learned a lesson (he thinks), a bitter and hard one—you cannot trust anyone. He plans never to be so naïve and gullible again, presumably because it made him feel foolish. Perhaps even that embarrassment, which his friends certainly would know about, is part of the impetus for his vow never to trust anyone, even his closest friends, again. It is clear that her betrayal signals to him that if someone as important to him as she was could leave, so, too, could his friends. In effect, he is leaving them first.

This song, which helped launch Haggard's career, is significant for that reason. It is a failed relationship song; such songs make up much of Haggard's repertory. It also indicates a deep-rooted bitterness about love relationships, common to many songs at this time.

Haggard captured the meaning and significance of many themes and issues that preoccupied country music in the past. His continued involvement in the industry means that these issues never entirely disappear, though they may reappear in slightly different guises.

❋

These singers and their songs represent the past issues and preoccupations of country music. While singers such as Haggard still produce songs and still attract a wide audience, prisons and wandering are becoming less and less the focus of country music. The following chapters will detail the songs which reflect ongoing and current issues in country music.

Love Songs

An old joke about country music goes, "What happens when you play a country music record backwards? You get your wife back, you get your dog back, you get your pickup truck back. . . ." The idea, of course, is that country music is about losing, about crying in one's beer over the mistakes one has made. And much of country music is about loss. But it is much too simplistic to suggest that country music is only concerned with losing your spouse and that all such songs are the same. If many country music songs are about that circumstance, such songs do remind us of the dangers of not loving well. But each song of loss has a different point of view. Some songs suggest that the loss could have been avoided, that it was the loser's fault. Some suggest that the one who lost could not have prevented it, that he or she misunderstood the unfaithful nature of the person he or she loved. Sometimes the songs of loss are positive—one grows stronger through realizing one can be independent and alone. Sometimes they even celebrate loss, as in "Thank God and Greyhound You're Gone."

It is clear, then, that of the themes country music most commonly offers as something to share, the theme of love predominates. This includes not only songs about lost loves, but all songs about love and relationships.

Country music is about handling the problems of everyday life, so it is not surprising then that love songs are the most common country music lyrics. Love relations occupy and preoccupy everyone. Unlike the love songs of popular music and rock, country music does not dwell on fantastic, impossible dreams of love, nor on what one insider calls "teenagers in love" songs. Country music love lyrics focus on realistic love songs that attempt to show how relationships really are: that sometimes they fail, sometimes they are difficult; sometimes one falls in love with the wrong person, and sometimes one suffers from unrequited love. Sometimes it does all work out and everyone lives happily ever after. But not often.

The performers discussed in this chapter—Hank Williams, Sr., Tanya Tucker, and Reba McEntire focus on the theme of love in all its manifestations. Of course, many other important artists have sung about love, but each of these performers has contributed to country music in an important or unusual way.

Hank Williams, Sr. is without argument one of the great pioneers of country music. This was acknowledged when he was elected to the Country Music Hall of Fame in 1961, the year the Hall of Fame was founded, eight years after his tragic death.

Born as Hiram King Williams in Alabama in 1923, his life, though brief, nonetheless left an indelible mark on country music. As a child, he began singing in a church choir, as have many country music singers. His mother, known as a strong, independent woman, influenced him greatly. A church organist, she taught him about music, though he always gave credit to a black street singer (Rufus Payne, known as Tee-Tot) for teaching him chords and harmony. Ernest Tubb was an important influence on his singing as well.

In 1946, Hank met Fred Rose, of Acuff-Rose Music Publishing, and signed on as a songwriter. Hank's career took off in 1948 with the song "Lovesick Blues." As a guest on the Grand Ole Opry, he so electrified the audience that he became a regular in the lineup.

Unfortunately, alcohol and other drugs destroyed him. By 1952, his first wife had left him, the Grand Ole Opry had fired him, and his band refused to tour with him. He died shortly thereafter, passing away in the back seat of a car, on New Year's Day, 1953. Nonetheless, his songs have lived on. Though he died more than forty years ago, his records still sell, his fan club is alive and well, and he has influenced a new generation of country music performers, notably Alan Jackson. Everyone from Elvis to Fats Domino to Frankie Laine has played and recorded Hank's music. Tony Bennett's version of "Cold, Cold Heart" was a pop hit and made him famous, though the song is pure country. Huey Lewis and the News recorded Hank's "Honky Tonk Blues" on their rock album in 1984, a tribute to his cross-boundary, enduring influence on other singers.

Hank wrote and recorded nearly 130 songs. These have been recorded over 4,000 times and not one of his works has ever been out of print. Each New Year's Day, as a testament to his enduring popularity, radio tributes are broadcast throughout the world. His most recent fan club, which is now only two years old, has over 800 members and was granted a booth at Fan Fair in 1995, a rare accolade at a time when even living performers were unable to obtain booths due to a limited amount of space. Hank, more than most performers, contributed to making country music appeal to a national rather than regional audience. The president of his fan club says that had Hank lived, "we never would have heard of Elvis Presley."[85] Of Hank's talent, the fan club president asserts that only two or three other people have come close—Elvis, Patsy Cline, and Jimmie Rodgers. "No one else is in the ballpark," he says, "let alone the ball game."[86]

Hank Williams, Sr. was at the peak of his career when he appeared on the cover of Country Song Roundup, *1950.*

Hank's museum is in Georgina, Alabama and his fan club works toward securing memorabilia and artifacts for it. T-shirts, paintings and anything with Hank's likeness on it find favor among his fans. The fan club's newsletter keeps track of radio stations that play Hank's music still—some are in New York, but most are in Tennessee or Kentucky.

So fascinated are people with the legendary performer that recently Hank's life has been recreated in the play *Lost Highway,* which has met with great success. A movie biography, *Your Cheating Heart* (1964), starred George Hamilton. Other tributes are not so well received. Hank's son vetoed plans to charge fans $10 for a one-inch square of land near his father's grave.

Minnie Pearl (whose real name is Sarah Cannon), remembers working with Hank on the Grand Ole Opry. "I've seen a few stars capture an audience. The excitement of the charisma starts to build as the emcee begins the intro and works to a crescendo as the name is called. None did it as well as Hank."[87] While it may be impossible to identify his genius, Hank's music left an important legacy for country music; people began to take it seriously as a musical style.

Hank's legacy also includes his son, Randall Hank (Hank Williams, Jr.); a stepdaughter, Lycrecia; and, by court decree, a natural daughter, Jett Williams, who has spent much of her life trying to prove that she is Hank's daughter and is entitled to part of his estate. As one reporter put it, "Hank. . . . sang about a lot of heartache and broken dreams in his short, hard life, but even he would be hard-pressed to do musical justice to the story of his illegitimate daughter."[88] Perhaps his audience identified the authenticity in his songs; he sang about hard times and he had been through hard times.

Though people remember Hank as a sad, tormented man, his stepdaughter remembers him as laughing and jovial and says her childhood was happy and normal. Hank's sister writes about their childhood, growing up under the watchful eye of their hardworking mother in rural Alabama in the 1920s and 1930s. Their father, a World War I veteran, spent many years in a veterans' hospital. It was left to their mother to feed and clothe them during the trying years of the Great Depression. This left a deep impression on Hank and gave him a genuine appreciation for women. His sister remarks that Hank was a great songwriter because of his "ability to share his deepest emotions with others through music."[89] One songwriter would say, "Hank Williams, you wrote my life." But Hank wrote his own life, and his ability to do so meaningfully has influenced generations of country music singers and songwriters.

Don Helms, who played steel guitar in Hank's band, The Drifting Cowboys, says Hank's songs rang true. "They're about the average guy who works all day, stops on the way home for a cold one and then gets hell when he gets home," he says.[90]

Linda Ronstadt points out "on one hand, his songs were beautiful in their simplic-

DEAR CLUB MEMBERS,

THIS WILL BE OUR FIRST NEWSLETTER FOR THE HANK WILLIAMS
MEMORIAL CLUB, STARTED IN DECEMBER,1957. THIS CLUB WILL BE
RUN A LITTLE DIFFERENTLY THAN THE REGULAR CLUBS, IN THAT OUR
STAR IS GONE, BUT YET HE IS SO NEAR TO ALL OF US. THERE WILL
BE VERY LITTLE CURRENT NEWS; HOWEVER I WANT TO BOOST OTHER
STARS THROUGH THE CLUB. SO MANY OF THEM HAVE HANK AS THEIR
INSPIRATION THAT MAYBE FROM TIME TO TIME SOME OF THEM WILL SEND
US A STORY TELLING US HOW HE AFFECTED BOTH THEIR LIVES AND
AMBITIONS.

IN EACH EDITION WE WILL TRY TO FEATURE A STAR AND A DISC
JOCKEY, AND IF THERE IS ANYONE IN PARTICULAR YOU WOULD LIKE TO
SEE IN OUR NEWSLETTERS, PLEASE FEEL FREE TO LET ME KNOW AND I
WILL DO MY BEST TO GET THEM IN ONE OF THE FUTURE EDITIONS.

I WOULD LIKE TO ESPECIALLY THANK THE DJs AT KEVE HERE IN
MINNEAPOLIS WHO PLAYED SO MANY OF HANK'S RECORDS THROUGHOUT
NEW YEAR'S DAY. WE REQUESTED ONLY THAT THEY DEDICATE A PORTION
OF THEIR PROGRAMS TO HANK'S MEMORY, BUT THEY SEEMED TO PAY
TRIBUTE TO HIM FROM THE TIME THE STATION WENT ON THE AIR AT
5:45 A.M. UNTIL SIGN-OFF AT 5 P.M. OUR MOST GRATEFUL THANKS
TO ALL OF THEM.

THE ENCLOSED MEMBERSHIP CARDS ARE TEMPORARY ONES, PENDING
ARRIVAL OF THE OFFICIAL CARDS, WHICH SHOULD HAVE BEEN HERE BE-
FORE THE HOLIDAYS, BUT HAVE NOT AS YET ARRIVED. AS SOON AS
THEY DO GET HERE, I WILL SEND THEM ON TO THE MEMBERS.

SEE YA NEXT ISSUE,

Delores Merrill

* *

VERN WEEGMAN

ONE OF KEVE'S THREE DISC JOCKEYS, VERN WEEGMAN, JOINED THE
STATION IN APRIL,1956. PREVIOUSLY, BEFORE COMING TO KEVE, VERN
HAD BEEN A DJ AT WGNS, MURPHREESBORO, TENN.; KWAT, WATERTOWN,
S. D.; WTWT, STEVENS POINT, WIS.; KDHL, FARIBAULT, MINN.; AND
KBOK, WATERLOO, IOWA. VERN STARTED IN THE DJ BUSINESS IN 1946.
HE ATTENDED THE AMERICAN INSTITUTE IN MPLS. TO BECOME A DJ,
AND HIS FIRST JOB AS DJ WAS ON RADIO STATION WMSL, IN DECATUR,
ALA. AND THE NORTH ALABAMA NETWORK.

VERN WAS BORN AT DETROIT LAKES, MINN. ON APRIL II, 1922. HE HAS
LIGHT BROWN HAIR AND HAS BEEN MARRIED FOR ALMOST SIX YEARS. HE
PLAYS GUITAR, AND HIS WIFE, PATTI, PLAYS BASS AND GUITAR AND
SINGS WITH JAN AND HER COUNTRY COQUETTES AT THE FLAME THEATRE
CLUB IN MINNEAPOLIS.

YOU CAN HEAR VERN ON KEVE EVERY DAY BUT TUESDAY. HE IS A GREAT
DJ--BE SURE AND WRITE TO HIM; REMEMBER BY WRITING TO THE DJs
ON KEVE YOU MAKE THEM KNOW THAT YOU WANT TO KEEP AN "ALL--
WESTERN" STATION. VERN WILL ALWAYS PLAY YOUR REQUESTS, AND HE
NEVER NEGLECTS HIS FANS. HE IS A TRUE AND GREAT COUNTRY-WESTERN
DJ.   (BY COURTESY OF THE CHUCK CARSON JOURNAL)

First page of the initial newsletter of the Hank Williams, Sr. memorial fan club, December, 1957.

ity. They're very forthright and honest, but they're also a lot more complicated . . . than they seem to the average listener."[91]

Bill Ivey, director of the Country Music Foundation, says, "Historically, the single figure who was most important to country music . . . would be Hank Williams, mainly because of his songwriting. He was the first country song writer whose compositions reached outside the bounds of country music."[92]

Chet Hagan, a country music expert, puts it this way: "Hank Williams was nearly illiterate, but he had a genius, there's no other word for it, a genius for the native American language. His lyrics are masterful. As someone who has tried to put a few words to music in his day can tell you, he's the best."[93] Hank is also widely considered responsible for perpetuating country music myths of the performer as lone, tragic figure—the wanderer and the exile who knows too much to fit comfortably into mainstream, hypocritical society. Other performers acknowledge this. Waylon Jennings sings about his own trials and tribulations and asks, "Are you sure Hank done it this way?"

Hank Williams is an important figure because in the early days of the commercialization of country music, he made the music "natural." He was the one who helped it gain the acceptance of popular artists and managers.[94] Called "the hillbilly Shakespeare," his old-fashioned voice still managed to be popular among 1950s fans of pop and rock music.

His first publicly sung song was called "W.P.A. Blues," a protest song which won him a talent contest at the ripe old age of thirteen. Thereafter, however, he stuck mostly with love songs; he is best known for his songs about failed relationships. His strong mother gave him a deep respect for women; his working class background helped his audience identify with him. The fatalism of his music contradicted the dominant social ideals of the time. People knew there was a gap between the lives they lived and the ideology of the period that set up romance and family as the pleasant and happy center of personal life.[95] Hank understood about the changes in the American family during the 1930s and 1940s. "His extraordinary popularity, his success at introducing country music to new audiences and his influence on an astonishingly diverse range of popular music artists and genres all stem from Williams' ability to understand and articulate the blasted hopes and repressed desires of his audience," as critics Leppert and Lipsitz put it.[96]

Hank was among the first to sing about marital infidelity, to point out that it was among the possible failures or failings one might have in life. This was in direct contrast to the dominant social ideology and the expectation that men could and should not admit such things even if they did occur. As critics Leppert and Lipsitz point out:

> In an age of renewed racism, he created a music that underscored the connections
> between whites and blacks. At a time of upward mobility and cultural assimilation

for much of the working class, he affirmed his standpoint as a worker and an ordinary citizen. In an age of resurgent patriarchy, he lamented the schisms between men and women . . . and sought closer connections to women.[97]

I Ain't Got Nothin' But Time

Hank's most famous songs include, "I Ain't Got Nothin' But Time," a song in which he invites a woman to call him anytime she wants a little fun. He has plenty of time. He assures the woman not to worry as he doesn't have a wife. In the end, he advises the woman to look around and see the other men in the world. She has plenty of time, too.

The rather disspirited remark, "I ain't got nothin' but time," does not seem to be a very attractive conversation starter. When the speaker invites the woman to call him, it is because they are both failures, since they both have nothing but time.

When the speaker says he doesn't have a wife, the implication is that his wife has left him, suggesting some failure on his part. The "time" the speaker has so much of is a symbol of the emptiness and lack of direction he feels since his abandonment. His recommendation that the woman he is speaking to should also look around and discover other men seems to point to his inability to keep a woman, and to his acknowledgement of this failure. To keep and nurture a romantic relationship is identified as difficult if not impossible, not just for the speaker, but for everyone else as well.

A big hit for Hank, this song typifies the loser and failed lover that is ubiquitous in Hank's songs. The situation is unhappy, but like his mentor, Ernest Tubb, Hank, in his songs, refuses to descend to self-pity, but instead uses irony and sarcasm to make his point about bitterness and pain.

Cold, Cold Heart

"Cold, Cold Heart" details the plight of a man who tries hard to show a woman how much he cares for her and all she can do is suspect that he is up to no good. He plaintively wonders why he can't ease her doubts. He knows that in the past another man hurt her and she is suspicious of the motives of all men. He hopes for some miracle that will melt her "cold, cold heart."

Here, the speaker's frustration is apparent. He is paying for something he didn't do. The difficulty is the result of complexities inherent in any love relationship. It should be simple. Two people love each other, what more is necessary? But, as the speaker discovers, many life experiences interfere with the ability to create and maintain a love relationship. The speaker laments this experience, though at some level he must acknowledge that those same experiences are what make her who she is, the woman he loves.

The apparent simplicity—he wishes she did not judge him by the actions of other people—is actually of greater complexity and sophistication, calling into question our assumptions about the nature of past experiences. It seems simple—she should acknowledge that he did not hurt her and so she should trust him. But the two are stymied. Because of her past experience, she refuses to trust him. As other country music songs tell us, we must learn from our mistakes. If, then, she made the mistake of trusting someone in the past, it is only natural that she learn from this and be more careful about whom she trusts in the future. Unfortunately, the wisdom complicates matters and will eventually destroy the relationship.

The love song is strongly rooted in the tradition of country music. Love is never easy. The life experiences we have impinge upon it. The song also became a great pop success for Tony Bennett and helped provide a wider audience for a traditional country song.

Lost Highway

The song, "Lost Highway" describes the speaker's life of sin. The speaker is just a man on a lost highway. Gambling, drinking and the wrong kind of women put a man on this "highway." Hank assures us that the lost highway is a place where it is impossible to find freedom or renewal. Instead it is the road which leads to destruction. He concludes his song with the admonition to take his advice and avoid these things (gambling, drinking and the wrong kind of women).

"Lost Highway" could be called a celebration of the life of a rambling man, but celebration would be the wrong word. It is more of a lament. Hank subverts the idea of the free and easy rambling man and shows the cost.

The highway here is an allusion to the "wrong road" or "broad highway" ("broad" and "lost" even share sound in common), the road that leads to hell, as opposed to the straight and narrow way. It also plays on the American myth of the highway as leading to freedom, change and a chance to start over. This lost highway, we can be certain, leads only to destruction. The highway is lost, as is the traveler upon it. That many of Hank's songs end with pieces of advice, as this one does, seems to be simply a convention to explain why he is singing the song. Instead of merely lamenting his situation, he is validating the experience by using it as an example of what others should not do.

As the title of the play about his life, the song could be said to symbolize Hank's life. Almost eerily, the song suggests a tortured loner self-destructing, which is exactly what Hank did, in the back seat of a car heading down a highway.

Long Gone Lonesome Blues

"Long Gone Lonesome Blues" is another song about loneliness. The speaker's lover leaves him and he despairs. But he is as ineffectual in life as he is in love—he can't even manage to kill himself. He jumps in the river, but the river is dry. Other attempts to change or end this unhappy life are all equally futile.

The pathos here becomes almost bathos. But Hank does this deliberately, showing us that any exaggerated emotion can seem comic, except to one in the middle of feeling the emotion. The song reminds us that we can never really understand the way another person feels.

The song plays on the association we have with songs about failed love relationships. We expect them to be sad, we expect to feel sympathy and to feel unhappy with the speaker. In this song, even as Hank's plaintive voice invites us to feel his sorrow, we have the sneaking suspicion that he is overdoing it. We are right; the speaker is almost a caricature of the unhappy, mournful, jilted lover. The ridiculous length to which the speaker goes to signal his unhappiness slowly reveals to us the truly absurd nature of such exaggerated emotion.

The song is one many people strongly associate with Hank. It is about loss and powerlessness, two of the most painful situations one can find oneself in, but it is comic in a sense. The song captures one of the essential responses Hank has to painful situations.

These are only a few of Hank's songs. While they deal primarily with love and loss, they offer a variety of perspectives. The lyrics at first seem simple, but they signify much more complex and ambiguous situations than is immediately apparent. Such songs invite a serious philosophical questioning about their ultimate—though perhaps not ascertainable—meaning.

Tanya Tucker

One of the most important female country music performers, Tanya Tucker, sings about love relationships, but her songs—and her attitude—are as much about sexual liberation as they are about love. Her love songs, such as "Strong Enough to Bend" are as much about her philosophy as they are about heartache and doubt.

Tanya Tucker was born in 1958 in Seminole, Texas, and was only thirteen when "Delta Dawn" became an instant hit. She was considered the heiress apparent to another child star, Brenda Lee. Her performances seemed shocking as she tackled subjects no other "girl" singer had done. She also had a surprisingly commanding voice for such a small person. She was only nine when she came to Nashville and by the time she was sixteen, she had sung about illegitimacy, murder and sex.[98] Known as country music's "wild child" she is more famous for her offstage behavior than her music, though she has had over fifty hit songs and has released 29 albums. Tanya's appeal is in the way she connects with an audience that is or might want to be like her. She rebels against the country girl image that was pervasive in the country music industry when she first began singing, and she is appreciated for this.

Her notable affairs have included Merle Haggard and Glen Campbell, both twice her age. She attributes the failure of these relationships to the inability of such men to deal with an independent, strong woman. As a single parent, she has endeared herself to a working class audience, one populated with plenty of single moms, though some have criticized her for failing to see the problem with having an out-of-wedlock child. Called the "Texas Tornado," she appeared on the cover of *Rolling Stone* when she was fifteen.

Professionally, she has had her ups and downs. Always on the cutting edge of country music, she tried to appeal to rock fans by making a rock album, which was unsuccessful. Throughout the early 1980s, she did not have any hits. But by 1986, she had released another string of Top 10 hits, and has been intermittently on the charts since then.

Her personal life has had some troubles, too. In addition to an illegitimate child, she has been stalked by a fan, earned a reputation for being wild and rowdy, and has checked into the Betty Ford Center, though she maintains that she doesn't have a drinking problem. Her tough lady image is the side that even her friends and family see most often. She blames her tough, independent behavior for intimidating men.

She explains her perennial appeal to reporters and writers by saying that "people love to read about people like me. They don't like to read about people who never do anything wrong, never say anything wrong, have never been to a wild party."[99] However, her personal life does get in the way of her professional life. "I have a whole audience that really doesn't know my music," she says. "They know me as a celebrity, so to speak, a tabloid queen."[100] Though often criticized for her personal life, she is, as has been observed, "the first female in the historically conservative country culture to have become a major star with an open, free sexual image. And she's certainly breaking ground by facing motherhood without matrimony. And so the tabloids talk."[101]

In 1992, Tanya had a well-publicized argument with then-Vice President Dan Quayle over his comments about the television show, "Murphy Brown" and family values. "Who is Dan Quayle to go after single mothers?" she asked. "What in the world does he know what it's like to go through pregnancy and have a child with no father for the baby? Who is he to call single mothers tramps?"[102] She expressed hope that she could change his mind and make him realize what it is like to be a single mother.

Through it all, she has been adored by her fans, who call her Miss Tanya. Her reputation and fans are widespread—she has fans even in Romania. But she is criticized for being selfish and not giving her band its due on her records and and in performances, a mistake that would be deadly except that she's a twenty-year veteran and is otherwise a polished professional. Her fans are among the most loyal and she is wholehearted in her appreciation of them. She tries to use her fame and popularity to influ-

✻

**Songs
of Life**

ence people to participate in causes she deems important; she currently supports the "Save the Eagle" campaign.

Strong Enough To Bend

In "Strong Enough To Bend" the speaker compares a love relationship to a tree. If a tree bends with the wind, it will not break, even during high winds. But if it is brittle or resistant, it will break. The song suggests that if lovers take a lesson from the tree, they will learn that for love to survive, they must also learn to bend. Instead of resisting the winds of change, they should bow to them.

The song exemplifies Tucker's philosophy about love. The comparison of love to a tree works so well as to be almost startling. The imagery allows us to see the association of a tree with a love relationship. One can even imagine the limbs of the "tree" cracking during an argument.

This song follows a long tradition of folk wisdom. Generations of parents passed such pieces of advice to their children. Now the speaker is evidently remembering and applying one such piece of advice to her own relationship. She is the one teaching her lover about the importance of following the wisdom. She is certain if they do as they should, and bend (cooperate, compromise), then their relationship will remain intact. This the speaker knows from her own experience of watching a tree, but it is also the result of a folk tradition mindset that looks for such analogies and allows such comparisons to be made, to be valued as well as valuable.

As one of Tucker's more recent songs, this philosophical lesson about how to make a love relationship work was successful enough to ensure that Tucker still knows what her fans want to hear and is still popular enough to sell plenty of records.

One Love At A Time

In "One Love At A Time," the narrator describes the difficulties of loving two men at the same time. She is afraid to fall asleep because she might say something that would give the show away; she can't keep their birthdays straight and so on. She describes how guilty she feels and how she needs just one love at a time ("that's all I can handle").

The song is sung at such a slow pace with such lament in the singer's voice that it is not immediately apparent that this is a funny song. The contrast between the slow, haunting melody of the song and its actual content is what makes the song enjoyable. It is not tragic in any sense; the speaker never actually loses one lover or the other. The worst thing that happens is she loses a little sleep out of pure paranoia. We feel she is getting what she deserves. Not only do we feel no sympathy for her plight, we are, if anything, jealous of it. It is hard to imagine having two wonderful men impossible to choose between when it is difficult enough for an ordinary person to find one.

While the singer's mournful voice invites us to commiserate with her, the most we can do is laugh at her. This is in a beloved tradition of country music, setting up a situation to seem tragic when it is really comic. The pleasure comes from realizing the dichotomy of comedy and tragedy—and then realizing that they aren't that different. We are invited to see, that with a few minor changes, "One Love At A Time," could actually be a sad song.

The song showcases Tucker's flexibility and allows her the chance to poke fun at herself and the persona she cultivates. Such a song helps to alleviate the overall serious, contemplative nature of Tucker's songs, adding an element of fun to her repertoire.

Would You Lay With Me In A Field Of Stone

In "Would You Lay With Me in a Field of Stone," the speaker asks her lover if he would perform a number of feats for her, if only she asks, including laying with her in a field of stone, but also encompassing going away to another land and walking a thousand miles (over burning sands, no less).

This is the mirror image of songs that detail what the speaker would do for love. Here instead the speaker asks another what he will do for love. The feats, straight out of romance, are outrageous, though the speaker offers them seriously enough. Yet we all know that such will not be asked of us, nor will it be given.

The song invites us to look at the components which make up romantic love—or our idea of romantic love, and perhaps reevaluate or analyze these ideals. On one level, the song simply asks us to accept such acts, that such actions might be taken if we loved well or truly enough or if we were loved well and truly enough by another. On another level, the song asks us to question what we mean by these acts, and how these prove love. What, in fact, do these acts symbolize? We are asked to ponder the connection of such feats to true love.

This is a signature song for Tucker, one that is exclusively identified with her. She first sang it before she was out of her teens, and its explicit references to sexuality (by a female singer, no less) caused quite a stir. The song is also significant, for it refers to the connection between sex and love that is a feature of many of Tucker's songs.

What's Your Mama's Name, Child?

"What's Your Mama's Name, Child?" describes a man who came to Memphis thirty years ago, looking for a woman. No one paid attention to him, so he resorted to asking children, "What's your mama's name?" Twenty years ago, we learn, the man was put in prison for a month for asking a child this question, and offering a bag of candy for a reply. Finally, as an old man ("last year"), he died and a letter was discovered in his belongings, from a woman in Memphis, who wrote that she has had his child.

The haunting melody of this song keeps the listener engaged until the "secret" is revealed. One imagines from the beginning that the man is looking for a woman, his former lover, but one only realizes at the very end that he has been searching unsuccessfully for thirty years. Upon notification of his fatherhood, he doesn't run away (which is what we might expect) but instead attempts to locate the mother and child. The futility of his quest is made more poignant because of his wish to do right by the mother and child.

This is one of a series of tragic ballads that Tanya Tucker has sung. The element of surprise keeps one interested the first time through, but the layers of meaning keep one returning. After one has successfully pieced together the story, one is aware of the series of interactions and misunderstandings that must have taken place to allow this to happen. In addition, one must wonder at the obsession of the man. Is it continuous, or is it brought on only occasionally, perhaps when he has been drinking and feeling maudlin? We can never know. What we do know is that he feels love, regret and pain, and that the lost lover and child occupy his mind and heart.

This is another signature Tucker song, first recorded when she was a young adult. It deals explicitly with illegitimacy, and was surprising at the time of its release. Now, it has gained layers of meaning as Tucker's own life has mimicked some of the events related in the song.

Tanya Tucker sings about love from a variety of perspectives. Though she does not sing solely about romantic love, it is her primary theme. She sings about lost love, failed love and happy love. She imagines herself in a variety of situations and shares these imaginative stories with her audience. Though she approaches the theme of love in many ways, the interaction of love and sexuality is a major concern for her, as it is for her audience.

Reba McEntire

While Tanya broke barriers about acceptable behavior in a country music performer, Reba McEntire has moved "back to the basics." Born in 1955, near Kiowa, Oklahoma, the daughter of rodeo followers, Reba wanted to sing even as a child. She remade several Patsy Cline hits but at first she made little progress with a singing career. By the early 1980s, however, she finally found her own voice and became successful. Her romantic style, coupled with her active stage show, has made her very popular.

Reba is loved by her fans because of the message of her music and her ability to tackle delicate subjects (one of her songs is about a one night stand that results in AIDS). This phenomenally successful singer appeals to both men and women and her down to earth attitude is admired. She is currently the biggest-selling female recording artist in country music. For four years (1984–1987), she won the Country Music Association award for Female Vocalist of the Year.

She has become a television personality, an actress and an investor, and bridges many different forms of show business. Recently, she starred with Kenny Rogers in

She plans to open restaurants and has
sponsored a guns for tickets tour, in which fans could turn in handguns to law en-
forcement officials and receive tickets to one of her concerts in exchange. She is a
spokesperson for Frito-Lay, plans to represent other products, and her image appears
on a Visa card. Like former president Jimmy Carter, Reba has worked with Habitat for
Humanity. Her most recent house-building project for Habitat was constructed with an
all-female crew.

She admits she is extremely competitive and ambitious, interested mostly in her
profession. Filling the traditional role of women is of no interest to her. As she has
achieved success and greater control of her career, she has expanded her song selection to include songs about battered women, divorce, widowhood and prostitution.
"I'm trying to sing songs for women, to say for them what they can't say for themselves," she told a newspaper reporter, "but I'm trying to do it for the 1980s and
1990s,"[103] referring to the way in which Loretta Lynn and Tammy Wynette sang songs
for an earlier generation of women. For this reason, it is important that she engage her
female fans, she thinks. They are the core buying audience, and she feels more comfortable with them now than she has in the past. "I just try to be honest, to be open
and not uppity, not sexy, not trying to steal their boyfriend or their husband—I got
one of my own."[104]

She still thinks it is as tough for a woman breaking into country music as it ever
was. By the early 1990s, the country music scene had swung back to embrace its
macho roots, thereby making it more difficult for female country music performers to
break through.

She remarks that over the years, mishaps on stage have occurred—her throat has
gone dry, she has forgotten words, tripped over microphone cords, "but they love
you if you're honest . . . if you try to hide it, they'll crucify you."[105] When such honesty
has failed to come across to the audience, she has been severely criticized in the
press. One reviewer said she "has been afflicted with the Whitney Houston Syn-
drome, the unexplained disease that makes spectacular vocalists blow their talent on
lame music" and that her showmanship was as stilted as her music. She was criticized for "running quickly through a rehearsed speech about childhood memories,
musical influences and career milestones, [with] all the genuineness of a carnival
barker."[106]

Her theatrics, too, have threatened to overshadow her talent. As one writer puts it,
"she should be commended for trying to take country music away from hay bales,
cornfields and wagon wheels, but at times the concert came off wooden and preten-
tious."[107] Still, her concerts reflect her stated goal of trying to make her appearances
entertaining spectacles, as well as opportunities for her fans to hear her live.

Her late 1994 single, "She Thinks His Name Was John," about a woman who is dying of AIDS, is the first and most poignant song about AIDS to reach a mass audience. Radio stations had immediate, sometimes overwhelming, responses to the song, almost all of them positive. "We felt it important for us to play it," one disk jockey said, "but we also thought it was a hot record."[108]

Reba's success has taken an odd turn. At Cowboys La Cage in Nashville, a nightclub with a stage show each evening, she is impersonated by David Lowman, who from some distance away looks a lot like her. The show of female impersonators celebrates country music performers. But the actors say they aren't poking fun at the performers. "When I do Reba, it's on a very serious note," David says.[109]

He Broke Your Memory

In "He Broke Your Memory," the speaker tells us that she treasures a former lover's memory just as if it were a precious thing, like a china cup, and that, like a china cup, she keeps it safe. But an accident happens. She meets another man who breaks the memory by holding her a little too tight.

The song is interesting because of the treatment of the memory as an object — something to be treasured, something to be broken — and the consistency with which the speaker uses this metaphor. We don't learn anything about the new man or the old one; we don't even know how the speaker feels about anything. All we know is the memory and that it is broken. But this is sufficient for the purpose of the song. Other details are extraneous. We are expected to focus only on the idea of memory as a thing and on how this metaphor functions in the song.

In this case, an event that would otherwise cause sorrow (the breakage of a treasured object) actually causes happiness. The speaker approaches the subject seriously, however. She is apologetic, almost hesitant, to admit to the breakage, as if she isn't quite sure how she feels about it or what it means yet. We know, however, that the one who broke the memory won't be chastised for it, but will in fact be rewarded.

This song shows how Reba uses imagery and metaphors to make concrete connections with internal, emotional events. This is in the larger country music tradition of using concrete analogies to clarify abstract or hard to define situations and emotions.

Somebody Should Leave

In "Somebody Should Leave," the speaker, part of a couple that sits in silence, describes how one reads while the other watches television. And love dies. The speaker points out that one or the other should leave since obviously being together is no longer beneficial. Yet it is not so simple, we learn. For instance, the speaker mentions the children. They can't do without their mother and their father can't do without them. Further, the speaker says they hate to admit it's over and must hope somehow it can work.

Yet, we realize that such inertia is not likely to lend itself to healing an endangered relationship. If one can't admit it's over, is it the fear of admitting failure that is the problem? If admitting there is a problem is impossible, then fixing the problem is equally impossible. The point that somebody should leave is so tentatively stated that a resolution seems impossible.

In this song, the tension is so well-balanced that it is impossible to decide what solution is best. It is impossible to decide what solution the speaker wants. One could suggest staying together, but obviously that is not working. The problem of who should leave is carefully expressed. The evidence is equally balanced. The fact that no one should leave is as clear as the fact that someone must leave is. The exquisite balance of each concern with an opposite concern shows just how impossible it is to make such a decision, and how impossible it is to allow the situation to continue.

This song is closely identified with McEntire, and was a big hit for her. The song captures the essence of McEntire's approach to the theme of love—that it is love's turning points that are most interesting and most worthy of comment.

Have I Got A Deal For You

In "Have I Got A Deal For You," the speaker meets a man whom she immediately identifies as a bargain hunter. The speaker tells him that she's willing to put on the market a heart that's almost new. She tries to "sell" the heart (and herself). She promises a lifetime guarantee, but warns that it's a one-time offer.

The idea of putting a heart on the auction block, so to speak, is not a new one. The song hints at a former love, who first used the heart. Though the speaker may legitimately wish to be healed from the original relationship and to move on, it is still just a line, a come-on. It seems clear that anyone will do.

A heart that is a bargain is not valued highly. The speaker—who we hope can find happiness—is artificially cheerful and confident. It is hard to believe in such cheerfulness and confidence. We can only assume that even if the bargain hunter takes her up on the offer, she will return too soon to this place with another deal.

The song is upbeat, uptempo, though not altogether happy. It showcases McEntire's vocal talent. From slow tear-laden songs, she can turn her voice up a notch to belt out a burlesque tune.

Only In My Mind

Like many of Reba's songs, "Only In My Mind," explores the relationship of a married couple whose love has changed and perhaps evolved over time. As the couple sit on a park bench watching their children play, the husband asks the speaker if she has ever cheated on him. He tells her to get the other man's memory out in the open. The speaker responds that she has cheated "only in my mind."

Though it is technically true that the speaker has not had an affair, we realize that the speaker feels more open and more comfortable with the other man than with her husband. The speaker finds herself blushing, perhaps from shame or from the memory of desire. She suggests it might be the heat. The situation is unusual. The husband does not become upset or jealous. He is merely concerned. Yet he assumes such an affair, if it ever existed, is over, and can be forgotten. But this is not possible, for the affair is very much present, and so we see the two talking at cross purposes. The speaker answers honestly, though guardedly, with no intention of breaking off the affair. She is simply surprised at her husband's perceptiveness. The dialogue is no dialogue, but two trains of thought running through the air together, each with a separate purpose and agenda—the speaker with a secret she must appear to be honest about, the husband with a facile belief that cheating happens once at night in a bed and then is over.

We realize that cheating can take place only in the mind but is no less cheating for that, though neither husband nor wife seems to realize this. Such cheating is just as damaging if not more so than any physical intimacy might be.

This song was another important hit for McEntire, and not only expresses her interest in the pivotal moments in a relationship, but showcases her tremendous vocal range.

Reba's dozens of hit songs deal primarily with love relationships. She focuses on those turning points in a relationship that can either make the relationship stronger or destroy it entirely. These pivotal moments engage her interest—and ours as well.

❋

Songs about love vary in approach to the theme. These singers-songwriters approach the topic from a variety of perspectives and show that country music has no one standard approach to the theme of love. The theme of love is extremely important to country music, since it must be faced by most adults. Country music doesn't offer platitudes about love; it doesn't offer an escape from the problems of love. It merely points out some different things about love. Sometimes we may take these songs as warnings, sometimes we merely identify with the emotion being shared.

Living

Country music has, at its roots, religious and philosophical beliefs about how life should be lived. This chapter will examine the theme that Jimmie N. Rogers called "living." This includes songs about how one lives, how one should live, and how one would like to live. It emphasizes religion, roots and pride in working hard. It elevates the country over the city and reinforces a "thank God, I'm a country boy" attitude.

As Zelda Fitzgerald once pointed out, "People live their lives by the philosophies of popular songs."[110] Country music imparts a religious and ethical message to its listeners. Ricky Skaggs, for instance, has created a video called "Silent Witness," in which country music performers give their testimonies and sing religious songs.[111] Country music is even used in churches to minister to people. At the Brown County Country Music Church in Nashville, Indiana, the music director programs old gospel standards like "Amazing Grace" but also includes contemporary country songs, plus some music written and performed by the church's own country music band. The country music flavor of the church services attracts people of all denominations. As the music director writes, "It's a blessing to know we can all worship together with at least two common threads, a love for Jesus and a love for country music."[112] The music attracts tourists, but the church has its regular congregation as well. The pastor says that it appeals to some people who may not have had positive experiences with churches in the past. The unique atmosphere allows such people to try again. Other country music churches are located in Kansas City and Nashville.

While some performers may debunk religious messengers and typical religious channels, they do not criticize the Christian message. Country music performers don't talk or sing about being Jewish, Muslim or any other religious persuasion. Thus, while Hank Williams, Jr. can get away with questioning televangelists, he doesn't question Christianity per se. Theirs is an unambiguous moral intimacy with God and community. Many country music performers record gospel music while having a secular career.

The love of Jesus, however, often gets mixed up with the love of women; the sacred and the secular are connected. In the song "Stand Up," religious words and concepts ("testify") are used to discuss worldly love relationships and most explicitly, sexual relationships. Another song, "Do You Want To Go To Heaven?" uses religious words and concepts to discuss worldly relationships.

Some performers capture this country music ethos and religious message—the "living theme"—extremely well. They are Charley Pride, Hank Williams, Jr., and Mary Chapin Carpenter.

Charley Pride

Charley Pride, the first African-American to achieve great success as a country music singer, is also one who sings about the country music ethos. His songs are about love and leaving, but also about Oklahoma mornings and rain on Highway 66. He was born in 1938, in Sledge, Mississippi, the son of cotton pickers. He sings mainstream country music; his first idol was Hank Williams. He learned to play the guitar at age 14, but originally thought he would be a baseball player. It was not until 1963 that Pride went to Nashville to seek his fortune. His first album went gold; many people were surprised when they discovered he was African-American. His gospel recordings show an African-American influence on his music, using instruments and vocal arrangements more usually associated with that tradition.

He now operates the Charley Pride Theatre in Branson, Missouri, and owns the Charley Pride Music Group, which publishes songs. His popularity is international; he just received the lifetime achievement award from the Great Britain Country Music Awards. After fifty-one albums, he still enjoys performing and appreciates the closeness he has with his fans.

Charley Pride made his first concert appearance in 1961. He had already been extremely successful in the recording studio. When he strode onto the stage, the mostly white crowd "began to applaud wildly. But as the athletically built singer emerged under the bright lights, the cheers collapsed into frightening silence. Somebody had forgotten to mention that Charley Pride was black."[113]

Pride later recalled the occasion. "You could hear a pin drop. . . . I told the audience, 'friends, I realize it's a little unique, me coming out here—with a permanent suntan—to sing country and western to you. But that's the way it is.'"[114]

Part of the problem was with the agents who promoted him. They were afraid that letting his race be known would severely damage his career so they did not release promotion pictures with the records they distributed. His fans, reasonably enough, thought he was white.

On January 7, 1967, Charley Pride made his first appearance on the Grand Ole Opry. History was made, for he was the first African-American to play there. Nervous about the prospect of singing for the crowd, Charley talked with them a bit and said, "I've got a lot of reasons to be happy tonight, real happy. But I guess my biggest reason is that I'm an American." This statement drew thundering applause and he was quickly accepted by the audience.

"I don't think of myself as the Jackie Robinson of country music," he says, speaking in baseball analogies that come easily to a man who intended to be a baseball player, "I'm not a pioneer. . . . I'm just trying to be myself."[115] As the son of a rural sharecropper, Pride explains, all the radio stations where he grew up played country music. So when he started to sing, naturally that was what he sang.

"Country is a basic American music. And its influence is spreading all over the world. Some people tell me I'm not supposed to sing country because I'm black, but why not? If I like it, it's my music, too."[116]

Pride considers his brand of country music to be based on the three elements of American music—country, gospel and the blues. Many of his more than 30 hit songs have crossed over to both pop and rhythm and blues charts, since his first million seller, "Kiss an Angel Good Morning" (1971). But Pride explains that he was unconcerned with crossing over. "Crossing over to whom?" he asks,[117] reminding his country music fans that they are the ones who count with him.

Pride has been acknowledged as a country music legend, whose warmth and sincerity, combined with his music, has touched people intimately. But Charley Pride warns that it is too easy for fans to expect an artist to also be an activist. Lots of people are looking for a savior, he says, "but if an entertainer goes too far with a philosophy or belief, then he's . . . a politician or a spiritualist or whatever."[118]

His attitude and philosophy are positive, energetic, and upbeat. He looks for such positive messages in the songs he records and performs. He is ranked number 13 of 20 top record sellers in the world, but he gets just as nervous performing as he ever did. He is humble and down to earth; he uses his clout to help others achieve success, including such singers as Ronnie Milsap and Neal McCoy. Still, he hasn't changed his style to keep up with fads.

Pride has something of an international reputation, singing in Ireland every year or two since he first appeared there in 1976. His 1994 album, *Classics with Pride* was a huge success in Britain and most of Europe, as well as Australia and New Zealand.

Though he has been welcomed by the country music establishment, it has been difficult for other African-Americans to achieve similar success. Cleve Francis, another African-American country music singer, recently left Nashville to return to his former career as a physician, while he had achieved some success, he has had a great deal of difficulty being accepted.

Is Anybody Goin' To San Antone?

Charley Pride's songs generally reflect an upbeat attitude, even though sometimes he does sing about loss and leaving. "Is Anybody Goin' To San Antone" is one of those songs about leaving. The speaker is hitchhiking along Route 66, rain dripping down his back. The circumstances are miserable; he's trying to find a ride to San Antone or

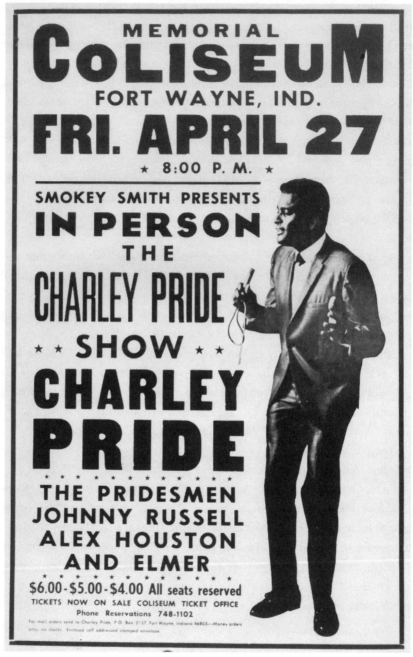

Even in 1970 all country music stars didn't appear on stage in blue jeans and Stetsons as this poster for the Charley Pride concert shows.

Phoenix—anywhere else is all right, too. He tells how sleeping outside in the rain is preferable to the situation he has been in. Nothing could be more uncomfortable than living with a woman he no longer loves, their home cold and unhappy.

The idea that sleeping outside in the rain is an improvement over shelter of any kind creates a picture of just how unhappy he was. Still, though the message is not upbeat or positive, the speaker is at least making changes in his life, changes he feels good about, instead of being trapped in an impossible situation like some of the lovers in other country music songs.

The song, while ostensibly about a failed relationship and the speaker's not-exactly-heartbroken determination to get on with his life, actually hearkens back to earlier songs that celebrate the traveler and the wandering life. The traveler here gives a reason for his traveling, but it still is a song concerned with the meaning of being alone and wandering. Even though travel has its discomforts, it is clearly preferable to a confining, responsible adult life.

As one of Charley Pride's best-known songs, this one combines a failed relationship motif with the theme of the traveler, which is still an important part of the living theme.

Tennessee Girl

In "Tennessee Girl," the speaker is hitchhiking across the country. He had been convinced that the promised land was somewhere ahead. The speaker has now realized that the promised land is actually the place he left behind. Now he's going to try to make his way back to his Tennessee girl, whom he plans to make his Tennessee wife.

The idea of appreciating what you have and the implied warning that if you leave it, it may not be there when you return, is a common one in country music songs about living. The wanderer motif is also important to country music, but sometimes wandering is seen as unfortunate. Sometimes, as with this song, wandering is an occasion for re-evaluating what has been left behind and learning to appreciate it.

While the wanderer motif embraces the idea of the rugged individual making his or her way through the world, this song shows us the falseness of that glamour. The promised land, vaguely realized, never materializes. How could it? The speaker does not know in the beginning what he wants, so he cannot hope to find it and he does not. But self-awareness helps him understand that he longs for his Tennessee girl—that is, he wants to return to the past, to the knowable and the known. In contrast to the very vague "promised land," we know exactly what Tennessee stands for: solid country values, faithful loving woman, all the necessary adjuncts to a happy, fulfilling life.

Again, this song uses the theme of love combined with the theme of traveling to make its point, a fine country music point about not abandoning what you have to go on a foolish quest for something you will never find.

**Songs
of Life**

"Oklahoma Morning" is a simple lyric song about how a beautiful day can make all of life's troubles seem unimportant.

The song celebrates a joy in being alive that is the hallmark of many country music songs that deal with living. It is, of course, a specifically Oklahoma morning being discussed here, not a New York City morning. A country morning, then, with its suggestion of clear blue skies and fertile green fields of corn is the one that works best to soothe one's cares.

The song suggests that simple appreciation of nature will put things in perspective. A beautiful morning, such as the kind you can get in the country, can cheer you up and put sunshine, as it were, back into your life. The song, with its positive, upbeat message reminds us that the simple things in life are best, and that an appreciation of one's natural surroundings can help one cope with one's daily struggles. The song also works with the idea that we should appreciate those transitory moments of joy that life does sometimes provide us. It further urges us to think about how we can create such moments in our lives.

The song is important as it conveys the traditional belief that country life is good for you and can make you happy in ways the city life cannot.

When I Stop Leaving I'll Be Gone

"When I Stop Leaving I'll Be Gone" is another song that describes an individual's inability to leave a relationship that is no longer working. In this case, the speaker wonders why, since some people manage to stay in love, his relationship doesn't work. With some self-disgust, he relates how he often leaves the relationship, only to return. It has happened so many times he has lost track. He knows the situation won't improve—they seem to need each other, but it doesn't work. Someday, he vows, he'll leave for good. Someday when he quits the process of leaving, he will actually have left, and will be gone.

The song flirts with irony and humor. The relationship must have something attractive about it, but the speaker's own disgust with the situation and with his behavior is almost comic, and brings to mind the Ernest Tubb/Hank Williams approach to failing relationships.

The detached sense of irony the speaker has is vintage country. He has stepped outside himself and can evaluate and comment on his own behavior, which he does with some bitterness. He seems resigned; if only he were a slightly different person, he wouldn't keep returning. His chagrin and ruefulness at his inability to end a failing, unhappy relationship speaks to an important country music perspective—plenty of things that seem as if they should be simple are not.

This song, detailing a failing relationship, continues in the wry, self-aware tradition of Hank Williams and Ernest Tubb, and provides a link between various generations of audiences.

Charley Pride's songs celebrate a mainstream attitude toward living, a unified attitude that celebrates home and faithfulness, but which also evokes images of traveling and leaving in contrast. Though he sings about love, he is almost always singing about an additional theme—the theme of living, as the country music culture embraces it.

Hank Williams, Jr.

Hank Williams, Jr., who wrote his autobiography in 1979 at age 30, inherited his father's mantle. Being a singer, he says, was his only option. He calls his father "country music's first authentic saint," in reference to his fans' fervent devotion to Hank's memory.[119]

Hank, Jr. spent his early years singing his father's songs to people who were willing to pay a kid to do it. He was heavily criticized when he tried to sing any other way. By the time Williams, Jr. was in his mid-twenties, however, drinking and drugs had debilitated him and he became almost a parody of himself. His fans would come to see him make a spectacle of himself and would bet on whether he'd make it through the concert or not.[120]

Marital problems, drinking problems and family trouble all gave Williams, Jr. the private life to make the public songs—songs about what a real country boy does. Though always a country music performer, he did make rock recordings under the name "Bo Cephus," which was the name of Grand Ole Opry ventriloquist Rod Brasfield's dummy.

Through it all, however, Williams, Jr. has been a shrewd observer of the country music scene. He points out that what makes country music different from other musical genres is the fact that the country singer is a "part of his audience, just a good ole boy or girl who happened to make it good and who never forgot how he or she came to be a star."[121]

Though country music had a hayseed image, he feels that the media outlets were what encouraged this. "When the Grand Ole Opry first started, the performers used to come to WSM's radio studios wearing three-piece suits. Before they went on the air, they changed into frayed overalls and checked gingham shirts."[122] He also points out that "the real problem is that the artist—me, for instance—has to straddle the fence between the smiling good ole boy in coveralls who learned to strum the guitar on the lower forty, and the professional businessman in a three-piece suit and a Yale education, who can figure cash-flow for the next five years and knows more about small print than a miniature Bible salesman."[123] He says that "we have strategy meetings . . . .

we discuss product—that's the music—packaging and marketing strategies. We discuss giant paper cutouts, press parties and trade magazine charts . . . . We worry about our managers, our publicists, and our fans. Sometimes we worry about the Internal Revenue Service and we decide to become professional wilderness guides or some other obscure profession. But we never do."[124]

Like Waylon Jennings and Willie Nelson, Hank Williams, Jr. doesn't like the Nashville country music establishment and has butted heads with many industry executives over his career decisions. He is perceived as a little high-handed, according to industry insiders.

"He was different after he fell off the mountain," one music programmer said, referring to an accident that crushed Hank's skull. His "rowdy friends" persona dates from that period—the late 1970s. His signature song, "All My Rowdy Friends" was adapted for the N.F.L.'s 20th anniversary season in 1994, but Williams has actually received little radio airplay in recent years. In the late 1980s and early 1990s, Williams failed to appear at numerous concerts, or appeared at others while drunk. In some cases, he would insult the audience. This caused many promoters to turn to other performers. Many refused to handle his shows. Even though radio stations play little of his music, he still sells many records. A hard core, loyal fan following awaits his releases with delight. Hank's fan club seems to thrive. He has had nine albums on the country music charts at the same time. To explain his success, regardless of his knack for offending fans and failing promoters, one recent magazine article gave ten reasons why people love Hank, Jr. The reasons include his father's legacy, his childhood career, his battle for an identity and his larger-than-life persona.

In 1985, Williams, Jr. won Video of the Year awards for "All My Rowdy Friends (Are Coming Over Tonight)," from both the Academy of Country Music and the Country Music Association. He released his 50th album when he was only 36 years old. In 1990, he was nominated for and won an Academy of Country Music award for a duet, "There's a Tear in My Beer," with his father. This duet was electronically created by dubbing Hank, Jr.'s voice on a Hank, Sr. track.

In 1990, however, Hank, Jr. was still allowing alcohol to affect his performances. This irritates many members of the country music culture because while rock stars can get away with outrageous behavior, country music performers are expected to have better manners and to treat an audience with respect. But, as one critic points out, "he seems hell-bent on self-destruction."[125] Although Williams himself credits his accident with making him rethink the path he was on, others agree that he has decided to continue along the same dangerous road his father took.

Hank, Jr. also came up with a Desert Storm song. Columnist Mike Royko says, "We should all be grateful to him for his patriotic outburst. The song is so awful that it might forever put a deserving end to the writing of patriotic war songs."[126] Rokyo quotes

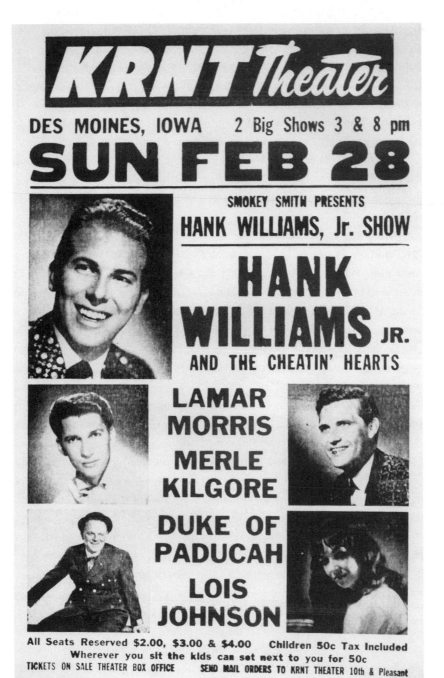

Touring shows usually included a mix of acts which appeared before the head-line star, as this 1967 poster for the Hank Williams, Jr. show indicates.

some of the more memorable lines — "You can take that poison gas and stick it in your sassafras," and "Yeah, I'd like to find out just how fast those camels can run." Royko also points out that though Hank was old enough to serve in Vietnam, he didn't.

Williams' 1990 album release, *America: The Way I See It*, drew mostly negative reviews, though some of the critics found themselves agreeing with the lyrics. The album had a forerunner — the song, "A Country Boy Can Survive" — which, with its survivalist credo, can seem chilling in this decade. His album, called a "self-righteous diatribe" is filled with conservative, anti-ethnic rantings that do appeal to some country music fans. Nonetheless, Hank is best known for his "country boy" songs — those songs that celebrate being from the country.

Family Tradition

"Family Tradition" is a personal song about Williams, Jr.'s life. He describes his self-destructive ways, like his drinking and smoking, and says that he got them from his father. Some of his "kin" disapprove of him and they ask how and why he has to live out the songs that he has written. He responds that it is the "family tradition."

Though the song has a rowdy, hard edged beat to it, it is a song with some bitterness. While Hank, Sr.'s legacy has been a blessing to Hank, Jr., it has also clearly been a curse; while it may have opened doors, Hank shows how it also left behind some unpleasant reminders.

"Family Tradition" plays on our understanding of family traditions as innocuous and even healthy events or beliefs held by a group of related people. In this case, the family tradition is a destructive heritage, a painful way of life. The song also has the belligerent tone often associated with songs celebrating rugged individualism. For, even as Hank, Jr., is caught up in this deadly cycle, he insists that damnation or salvation is in his own hands. The song makes one think of the family traditions one might have that are equally unhealthy or even dangerous.

As a popular Williams, Jr. song, this one explains the unenviable position of the singer, whom we might otherwise envy. The personal portrait reveals the pain and conflicts in his life, and, like the country music most appreciated by fans, is authentic and real.

Dixie On My Mind

In "Dixie on My Mind," the speaker is "up North" and he misses southern things — Jack Daniels whiskey, for example. He has obviously been in search of a better life, but he's had all he can take. He'd like to leave but he's stuck. He contrasts "Dixie" with the "Big Apple," and the big city loses by comparison. It is full of money-hungry, unfriendly people; it is restrictive, and worst of all, the people there don't know how to party. There's no hunting or fishing — just a few squirrels.

"Dixie On My Mind" celebrates country culture, specifically southern culture. Country living is preferred to city living. When the speaker finds himself stranded in a city, he longs to return home. The longing to return home is a common one in country music, but this is further emphasized by contrasting two ways of life and elevating one above the other. Several bars of the melody from "Dixie" are played at intervals throughout the song, which again stresses the southern orientation and the wish to return home.

The song identifies those things that a "country boy" values. For the most part, these are typical activities like hunting, fishing and partying. The speaker's frustration at being unable to return home makes him sarcastic about city life, but also, perhaps unintentionally, ridicules that same country boy mindset by showing the limited perspective available to him.

The song was popular and received a fair amount of radio play. More importantly, it sets up the contrast between city and country life that so preoccupies Williams, Jr.

The American Dream

"The American Dream" does not share the uncritical adoration of other Williams, Jr.'s songs. Here, he complains of too many lawyers, of sports figures who make millions of dollars, ministers who exhort—or extort—money from their listeners. He complains about how no one has time, and everyone is stressed. He criticizes the Republicans who supposedly cut the budget, but increased taxes. Nothing gets solved, the speaker says, we just go round and round. He points out that much time is spent trying to get things we don't really want or need, and then trying to keep these things. People go crazy living the American Dream.

Instead of a simple celebration of "American" values, Williams asks us to reexamine what we think is important and make our priorities based on things other than status, power and material things.

As a departure for Hank, Jr., this song shows how the perceptions of a country boy can be shrewdly analytical. The point is that these supposedly smooth and urbane operators (evangelists, politicians) aren't fooling anyone—most especially those people to whom they give the least credit. As a social commentary, it catalogs a fairly typical list of crimes, but it works to show that even the stereotypical redneck country boy can understand the social and political issues that he is neither expected to understand nor care about. Further, the song celebrates the country living theme in the sense that it celebrates the country boy—and his listeners—who are astute and aware. It also suggests that by being aware, one can act in one's best interest, not relying on others to guide or direct one's life.

As a song that criticizes the establishment, it won favor among many fans. Further, it celebrates the common sense beloved by country music culture.

In "A Country Boy Can Survive" the speaker says that bad things happen in the city. He tells the story of a friend who was killed by muggers over a small amount of money. In the country, however, people grow their own food and make their own wine, go hunting and fishing and basically survive by living off the land.

The song has an apocalyptic vision; terrible things will happen soon, but country folk—survivalists, actually—will survive. People who are foolish enough to live in cities and who never learned to trap won't survive. They'll deserve their fate because they weren't prepared.

As a survivalist credo, the song has actually taken on an ominous subtext that probably did not exist when it was first released. While it points out the dangers of city life, in contrast to the simpler country existence, the main point of comparison is one of preparedness. The country boy can live off the land, can hunt, can fish, and furthermore, can conduct vigilante justice if necessary. As a comparison of country and city life, it clearly favors country life, but the rather unrelenting vision of urban decay and country utopia is disconcerting.

This song was extremely popular on release, criticizing crime and injustice while celebrating rugged individualism. It is extremely typical of Williams, Jr., and reflects the country music appreciation of the strong individual able to take care of himself and all that belongs to him.

Hank Williams, Jr. has established himself as the spokesperson for country living, the country music ethos. In attempting to differentiate himself from his father, he has focused on the theme of living, rarely writing about love. He discusses living frankly, especially as it is played out against the backdrop of the Williams legacy.

Mary Chapin Carpenter

Mary Chapin Carpenter says that folk music performers influenced her more than honky tonk performers. She and others like her, including Suzy Bogguss, appeal to audiences' minds and hearts. Carpenter originally had pop intentions, but country music adopted her first and she has never regretted it.

Born in 1958 in Princeton, New Jersey, she spent much of her early career in Washington, D.C. Nashville stardom surprised her, for she knew little about country music when she first became popular. Her degree from Brown University is in American Civilization. After graduation, she began working as a folk singer, and soon, like many country music performers, developed an alcohol problem (which she eventually overcame). Her songs speak to country music ethos: loss of love, weary women, lonely dreamers, and others. Carpenter's first album sold respectably. Her second album, *State of the Heart* stayed on the charts for more than 30 weeks. While she enjoys performing, she has found the spotlight difficult. Though her music is often sly and witty, she doesn't find herself at ease with crowds; her ability to communicate resides mostly in her songs.

As one critic says about Mary Chapin Carpenter: "[she] isn't a coal miner's daughter. She didn't grow up dirt poor in the backwoods. She doesn't wear a bouffant hairdo and there is no country twang in her voice."[127] She doesn't fit country music clichés. But then, neither does country music anymore. Carpenter has fused traditional country music with the folk movement of the 1970s to create her new sound. Her musical influences have been eclectic, ranging from opera to the Beatles to The Band.

As a songwriter, Carpenter uses the music to express herself. "I don't know why I write the songs I write," she says, "I don't know what the process is all about, yet I'm very aware when it's happening. . . . Your aim has to be true. You can feel when it isn't. It sounds false and it feels false."[128] Carpenter says that she knows a song is a success when people tell her it evokes and touches their feelings, too.[129]

The feelings she describes are hers, but they transcend the personal and become universal. One critic says, "What she really turns out is pop and soft rock built upon country themes."[130] Carpenter doesn't argue; she says she is just happy there's a place for her in country music. "Her songs—almost always confessional, whether they're mournful, contemplative or angry—rely on country idioms even as they bend the genre."[131] Carpenter is called the "urbane cowgirl." She points out that country music is not about what you look like, but "what you're saying and how you say it."[132] Carpenter attributes her success to the changing nature of the country music audience. A typical fan, she finds, is likely to be educated and live in a big city.

Her album, *Come on, Come on*, deals with similar themes: women who are caught between traditional and contemporary roles. One critic says, "average women seldom steal the fire. It's the ones with all the drama, the warriors and the victims, who end up in the newspapers, the television movies and the country songs: the battered women, the thieves and adventurers, the defiant ones. But Mary Chapin Carpenter's [music] is a testament to the women who don't usually make headlines."[133]

She writes and sings about housewives, kid sisters, sales clerks and other average women. Without patronizing or belittling these women, Carpenter is able to gave her characters dignity and emotional appeal.

He Thinks He'll Keep Her

"He Thinks He'll Keep Her" is about a woman who does everything she is "supposed" to do. She marries at 21; she makes her husband's coffee, his bed, his meals. She has singlehandedly (well, almost) created a perfect family, so "he thinks he'll keep her." (That tag is from a Folger's coffee commercial in which a patronizing husband's delight in finding that his wife has brewed a good cup of coffee is expressed in these words). The wife leaves her husband and goes to work, as a typist, for minimum wage.

The song examines the traditional attitudes toward such women. It praises the woman's ability to identify her unhappiness and then escape from it. Still, the escape has its problems. Minimum wage won't keep a roof over her head, and even though she has been working hard all this time, she has never been compensated for it. Her skills have no real business world value, though we know how important her "job" was. The unfairness of the entire situation slowly sinks in, though Carpenter merely mentions the facts; she doesn't tell us we should be outraged by them.

The storyteller uses an understated tone to describe the situation and relate the events. Instead of being angry or bitter or happy, the speaker keeps her opinion out of it. It is clear, however, that we are expected to see the ironies apparent here. We are supposed to dislike the husband whose expectations of his wife are so dismally small and yet so incapable of being fulfilled. But the patronizing husband, of whom we know little (the song isn't, after all, about him) is a place-filler, not a husband. He reflects society's expectations, nothing more; just as societal expectations dictated her actions (up until now), so they have dictated his—his actions, his attitude, his words. All this, however, has changed, and just as she has taken responsibility, so must he (and so must society). In a way, this is another failed relationship song, but what has failed is the society that set up such impossibly limiting expectations.

This catchy tune is one of Carpenter's most recent hits, showing that she is not likely to slow down any time soon. While the song questions fundamental assumptions about the arrangement of the world, society, families, and so on, the questions are apparently being asked by many country music fans, given the popularity of the song. While it is overtly about women's issues, the underlying theme is about living, how we expect to live and how we expect others to live.

I Feel Lucky

"I Feel Lucky" is one of Carpenter's most successful songs. It's about a woman who reads her horoscope, sees that she has a bad day in store, but refuses to let this stop her. Her inner instincts tell her she is lucky today and she is; she wins the lottery (the jackpot is $11 million). Later, she finds herself in a bar with contemporary country music singers Dwight Yoakam and Lyle Lovett vying for her attention.

The absurd improbability of this song is only matched by the speaker's glib smugness about it all. The song makes you want to go out and buy a lottery ticket; it urges you to listen to your instincts. The happy, exuberant self-confidence of the speaker is infectious.

As a country song about living, this one is more upbeat and positive than most. It suggests a philosophy of life that relies on trusting one's instincts and doing one's thing, without worrying what other people think or say. These are certainly messages very common to country music, but the speaker here is not a defiant rugged individualist so much as a smug (and lucky) ordinary person.

This is a very popular hit for Carpenter, partly because of its upbeat tempo, partly because of its absurd improbability and partly because it confirms what country music culture believes about self reliance in the face of doom saying.

The Hard Way

"The Hard Way" is about a troubled relationship. The speaker asks her lover to remember that keeping their relationship intact hasn't always been easy, and that their love has always been earned the hard way. If they can remember their past and recognize that keeping a loving relationship in working order is often difficult, perhaps they can succeed.

The "hard way" is a phrase that echoes with allusions to country music culture which praises hard work and commiserates about hard times. Though Carpenter is not from a poor family, her message seems authentic because she is seen as personally having difficulty with love relationships. This is important to country music fans who might not accept a message about hard times from a singer they did not perceive as having gone through them.

This song is notable, because it easily transforms its meaning for the listener. People can interpret it in different ways—as a reassurance that hard times end, that hard work is rewarded, that everyone has hard times, or that the hard way is the only worthwhile way of getting or earning something. The song works on many different levels, and only on the literal level is it about a troubled relationship.

This enormously popular song is important because it speaks to the country music fan. One message that the country music living theme presents is the message that life is full of hard work. This song, because it can be interpreted in many ways, shows the various meanings of hard work to the audience. Because it seems authentic, it is accepted as a believable message from a believable singer/speaker.

Never Had It So Good

In "Never Had It So Good," the speaker knows the relationship she is in is over. Her lover's old girlfriend is back in town, and he has never had it so good. The speaker, on the other hand, has never had it so bad. The speaker consoles herself with the thought of how the old girlfriend will dump him again, and the speaker, who will be vindicated, won't even bother to answer the phone.

The speaker knows there is a difference between herself and the old girlfriend. She realizes that she cannot compete against the woman, and further, she has no intention of trying. This does not mean that she does not feel pain from the loss of love and the rejection in favor of one who is, in some unstated way, superior. Still, the song ends with the defiant speaker predicting that the old girfriend will disappear again. And she is resolved that she won't be waiting around for this to happen. She will have recovered and perhaps moved on to other things. Even if she has not, her pride will serve to shield her from the temptation to began the relationship again. Thus, what is an unhappy situation has been transformed into one of triumph for the speaker.

The "it" continually referred to in this song is deliberately ambiguous. For the speaker, "it" might mean her life circumstances (her life has never been this bad), or "it" might refer to love and affection (she's never had as much love and affection for the man as she does now, when the relationship is over.) This ambiguity means that both readings are acceptable, depending on how one wishes to interpret the words. This failed relationship is the direct result of external interference—another woman has come and stolen the speaker's lover away. The speaker doesn't really blame the other woman; it is the wayward lover who is at fault. Like many other songs about failed relationships, this one discusses the grief and pain one feels, but, while acknowledging the grief and pain, the speaker presents a slightly unusual philosophy of life. She will get over the pain and she will refuse to take back the man who caused the pain.

As Carpenter's first big hit, this song established her as a country music star, a situation she was not ready for, but which she has readily embraced.

Mary Chapin Carpenter's songs are imbued with folk, pop and rock elements, but she captures the country music feel in all of her songs. Some are more Cajun-inspired and some are more Appalachian-inspired as she is eager to use a variety of sounds in her music. Her slightly quirky philosophy of life and of living melds into the country music culture. In some ways, her way of thinking contrasts with country music culture, but often she presents merely a different way of looking at a belief that is commonly held dear.

❁

Issues about living sometimes have to do with religion and spiritual salvation or, more often, with living right, as defined by country music culture. Such songs have to do with the country ethos, that living as country or rural people do is the better way to live. Some of the songs just detail the ordinary events of common people's lives, with empathy and understanding. Songs about living are meant to be identified with, even if we all have not lived exactly the same experiences, and thus, it is especially important for the singer to be seen as one who has had these life experiences.

Women's Issues

The place of women in the family, the social world and the political arena has always created tension between the genders. This tension has been especially apparent in the country music field, which is a conservative, male-dominated one, and has only slowly and stubbornly changed. However, as women's roles have expanded in the world, so too has their representation in the country music industry expanded. Further, while female country music performers have voiced concerns about women's issues for several generations, only in the last ten years have a substantial number of female performers succeeded in the country music business with non-traditional messages. Although only recently have women been admitted to the business in large numbers, there have always been strong, independent female country music singing about their lives. For every Tammy Wynette "Don't Liberate Me, Love Me," there's a Suzy Bogguss "Hey, Cinderella." Several female country music performers see themselves as singing especially for women, about specifically women's concerns, women's issues. Others have played major roles in breaking down barriers against female country music performers and opening the door for others to follow. Some of these women are Loretta Lynn, Dolly Parton, and Suzy Bogguss.

Loretta Lynn

Loretta Lynn, another Hall of Famer, traveled with Patsy Cline and was protected and encouraged by her. Born in 1935, in Butcher's Hollow, Kentucky, she married Oliver Lynn when she was 14. With him she had six children. Her husband helped her launch her career and has always supported her. She is appreciated by her fans, for she has never forgotten her country roots. She is called the "queen" of country music and was considered the successor to Kitty Wells, who is still working. Reba McEntire is considered by many to be Lynn's heiress apparent

Lynn's first big hit, "Success," came in 1967, and since then she has had numerous top songs. She combines a traditional sound with progressive lyrics that retain a country foundation. She sang many duets with Ernest Tubb in 1964–1969 and later had a singing partner in Conway Twitty. He was impressed with her talent and helped guide her career. She was, she feels, extremely fortunate to have such important stars help her shape her talent.

Some of Lynn's songs celebrate country ethos—"Coal Miner's Daughter," for ex-

Shown here on a 1966 poster, Loretta Lynn and Conway Twitty recorded best selling hits and won Country Music awards for their duets during the 1970s.

ample—but others, like "Rated X," criticize social attitudes. Many of her songs, such as "The Pill," have been controversial and this never fails to surprise her, since all she is doing is saying what she thinks, and what other people think as well. "The Pill" was banned on radio stations across the country but Lynn managed to make it successful, for by the time the song was released, she was powerful enough to overcome programmer's objections to her choice of messages.

She is warmly regarded by her fans—she thinks of them as an extended family with whom she maintains a personal relationship. Her fan club consists mostly of women, for whom she is a role model.

The Pill

In "The Pill," the speaker is disappointed with her marriage. Her husband promised her a world he never gave her (and perhaps never intended to give her). Instead, he runs around while she stays home, like a "brooder hen." But now that she has the pill, things will be different. He had fun and she had babies; now she's throwing away her maternity dress. She plans to wear miniskirts and will make up for all those lost years.

"The Pill" is a straightforward, explicit description of how a woman's life will change (for the better) now that she has the pill. Feeling good will come easy now, since she has the pill. She will have the freedom her husband always had—and clearly that frightens him. This song's explicit discussion of sex for pleasure without the threat of getting pregnant caused a storm of controversy. It challenges ideas about roles and how women should behave, but most of all it celebrates the ability women will have to control their sexual and reproductive roles; she needn't even ask her husband if he agrees with her taking the pill.

While Lynn always expressed surprise that this song was controversial, listening to it even today can make one surprised at the blatant celebration of sexuality with no consequences, and reminds one that feminism would have been sorely limited if such a simple, reliable method of birth control had not been invented. Lynn celebrates sexuality here but mostly she celebrates the freedom the pill signals.

This song is important for historical reasons—as an extremely controversial song on an extremely controversial subject. That Lynn was able to convince programmers to play it shows the power she had by then attained through her ability to write and sing songs that touched the lives of a large number of people.

When The Tingle Becomes A Chill

"When the Tingle Becomes a Chill" details a troubled marital relationship. The speaker, who has not taken any drastic steps (yet) says that sometimes when her husband is asleep, she cries because she no longer feels the way she once did. She never meant to stop loving him, but she did. Now she feels unhappy and uneasy; she must pretend. Her body performs, but her soul is no longer engaged.

We can't help but feel sympathetic for the speaker and her situation. The description of mechanically making love gives us a hint of the distaste that the speaker herself feels. She is at a loss for an explanation; she does not know why this change occurred, and seems to have abandoned searching for causes. She is at the middle ground that exists between being content and taking action. We know she will soon start looking for solutions, and that will require leaving this otherwise good individual.

The speaker is blunt and straightforward about her concerns. What is clearly at issue here is that the speaker no longer finds her husband sexually attractive, and now she is faced with a passionless marriage (made more repugnant by the fact that she can hardly bear his touch) so perhaps she must leave him. Even now, songs about failing love relationships rarely touch on the fact that sexual desire often falters and this is what causes the trouble. Such a frank appraisal of sexuality and the importance of sexual relations in a marriage is unusual even now, but it is something the country music culture is ready to face and to discuss.

Like Hank Williams, who made a career out of discussing infidelity, Loretta Lynn has made a career out of discussing sex and related problems, though she herself probably wouldn't look at it that way. This song is typical of her blunt and straightforward approach. She challenges us here: if she is not afraid to talk about it, why should we be afraid to hear it, and perhaps talk about it ourselves?

Rated X

In "Rated X" the speaker criticizes what happens to divorced women. If a marriage doesn't work out, a divorced woman is "Rated X." She is talked about, and she can't have male friends. People call her a golddigger. This is wrong, the speaker says — everyone makes mistakes. The speaker says that friends' husbands will start hitting on a divorced woman. Other women will think she's bad and men will hope she is.

The speaker portrays all the indignities a divorced woman suffers. It is pertinent to note that she leaves divorced men out of the picture. Whatever particular troubles they encounter, they, at least, don't suffer the stigma of being "Rated X." This is especially nettlesome for women, whose reputation is what they are judged by, and a divorced woman's reputation is immediately considered soiled.

Though the issue discussed here is one that is less troublesome than it used to be, the song is still interesting in its depiction of the double standard that exists, which allows men to be judged by a different set of rules from women. Again, Lynn takes a view sympathetic to the plight of women. Lynn shows that she is at home discussing the ramifications of divorce, though she herself never went through it, and the prevailing view is not the one she accepts. She clearly sees that women's sexuality is at issue here and she defines the situation as such. She attacks the typical perception that a divorced woman's sexuality is out of control and that she is a threat. Lynn assumes that the last thing a divorced woman wants or needs is another sexual relationship. She also criticizes the assumption that being divorced somehow automatically makes one less trustworthy, so that even one's own friends act as if they must be careful. She finds such beliefs frustrating, if not disgusting.

The song, with its blunt discussion of divorce and desire, fits into Lynn's repertory of songs focusing on issues of particular interest to women. She examines all situations from the woman's perspective and is not concerned about the man's.

Coal Miner's Daughter

"Coal Miner's Daughter" is a song based on Lynn's childhood. There was always plenty of love, she says, and though they didn't have a lot, the bare essentials were provided. They learned to appreciate things of real value, like all the love they shared. To appreciate God was important, so the Bible was a household fixture. Working hard was also important, not necessarily because one got ahead that way, but because a solid work ethic indicated that the worker had good values. Finally, family members were expected never to complain about their situation, and to accept their lot.

This song is in the tradition of celebrating "country." The song not only divulges details of Lynn's upbringing, but gives important information about living "right" the way country folk do. The song emphasizes that Lynn is proud of her heritage, as proud as any blue-blood might be. This is a value important to country music—pride in one's roots.

Lynn has sung several songs about having a country upbringing and how it instills good values in an individual, but this is the most autobiographical, and, since it was the title of her movie biography, the best known. It captures the sense of pride not only in heritage, but pride in being poor, that somehow through being poor, she and her family were able to be better people than rich folk might find possible. She reiterates the message that since they had all they needed—love, the bare essentials—they were not aware of what they did not have. It is that awareness of what one does not have that leads to desire and trouble, but her family prevented such futile longings.

"Coal Miner's Daughter" is one of the most famous country music songs ever; even people who never listen to country music have at least heard the title. For this reason alone it is worth mention. As a song that celebrates country, and had great exposure, it also helped spread the message of country music.

Loretta Lynn focuses on women's issues. Sometimes these are concerns of special interest to women, as in "The Pill." Sometimes, she focuses on non-gender specific issues, such as divorce, but examines these issues from a woman's perspective. Her frank discussions of sexuality were controversial but refreshing to the country music industry, and now she is considered a living legend.

Dolly Parton

Certainly one of the most colorful women in show business, Dolly Parton is all about women and independence. Her sense of business is as sharp as that of rock queen Madonna. Of her persona, Dolly says, "I was always impressed with Cinderella and Mother Goose and all those things when I was a kid because we didn't have television or movies then. I kinda patterned my look after Cinderella and Mother Goose—and the local hooker."[134] Even Gloria Steinem celebrates Parton and her manipulation of stereotypes. Dolly was born in the Smokey Mountains of Tennessee in 1946, the fourth of twelve children. Although very poor, Parton had a happy childhood (owing at least in part to her own exceedingly happy disposition). She began singing and playing instruments while in school. After high school graduation, she moved to Nashville and lived with an uncle. In 1967, she began singing duets with Porter Wagoner and continued to do so throughout the seventies. After their breakup in 1974, Dolly went on as a solo act and in the following years has had many hits. Her "9 to 5" song and movie show her empathy with the struggles of working class women, while she also sings songs about loving and leaving. Some of her greatest songs are gospel or Christian country. Her religious songs are inspired in part because of her true life experiences. She tells the story of her "coat of many colors":

> I was probably about nine years old when my mama made me my little "Coat of Many Colors." I'll never forget running home to mama, crying my eyes out, saying everybody laughed at me, that my coat was nothing but a bunch of rags and we was poor. I never forgot what mama said to me. She said,"Dolly, we ain't poor. There's a whole lot of folks worse off than us. Now you wear your 'Coat of Many Colors' and you remember you're only poor if you choose to be." So that painful experience became a valuable lesson and a great blessing because it's what inspired me years later to write one of my favorite and most famous songs. "Coat of Many Colors" became a big hit and it's really amazing how healing money can be.[135]

Dolly has also ventured into film, with movies such as *9 to 5* and *Best Little Whorehouse in Texas.* Briefly she hosted a country music variety show on television. Dollywood, her theme park in Pigeon Forge, was created to help the economy in rural Tennessee where she grew up.

9 To 5

"9 to 5" is a song that expresses the frustrations of working women, especially those who are not professionals—clerks, secretaries, and others. The speaker bemoans

REGISTER HERE TO WIN . . .
A WEEKEND AT DOLLYWOOD
OR FREE CONCERT TICKETS

Hook's
Dependable Drug Stores
welcome

Dolly
PARTON

Dollywood.
You can win a trip for 4 to Dolly Parton's own theme park, DOLLYWOOD, located in the beautiful Smoky Mountains of Tennessee. This grand prize package includes tickets to DOLLYWOOD, tickets to the DOLLYWOOD Theatre, tickets to the Dixie Stampede, 2 hotel rooms for 3 days and 2 nights, plus $100 CASH. Runners-Up will receive 2 tickets to the Dolly Parton concert at the Indiana State Fair on Fri., Aug. 18th.

DWIGHT YOAKAM
and Clint Black

Live at the Indiana State Fair
Friday, August 18th

Tickets to the Dolly concert at the Fair are on sale now at all TICKETMASTER locations and the State Fair Box Office. Charge By Phone at 927-1482, 317-239-5151 or 800-284-3030.

RULES & REGULATIONS

1. No purchase necessary.
2. Winners must be at least 18 years of age.
3. Contest ends Thursday, August 10, 1989.
4. Winners will be notified by telephone.
5. Tickets do not include admission to the fair.

6. Ohio residents may mail name, address and phone number to:
   Hook's Advertising/Dolly Contest
   P.O. Box 19903
   Indianapolis, IN 46219.

Listen to the
gti-Business
Network
for more details.

Contests offering fans either free concert tickets or trips have long been part of country music marketing. An Indianapolis drugstore sponsored this 1989 contest whose winners either went to Dolly Parton's Dollywood theme park or to her concert at the Indiana State Fair.

working long hours, from 9 to 5, for little pay. She points out that she never gets credit for her ideas, she never gets promoted and the boss always blames everything on her. The speaker points out that she has dreams, too, and wants to get ahead.

In the movie, a group of employees get their revenge; since the movie and the song interact, the song is often seen as a defiant song, one that celebrates the put-upon workers taking control. In this way, the song works as a sort of wish fulfillment fantasy.

The song works as a sort of anthem for working women, to whom it mostly appeals. The speaker is a hard working woman who never gets adequate reward for what she does, but nonetheless, she keeps trying, which is in tune with the country music ethic. Further, the speaker is aware that she is being deliberately prevented from going anywhere in her job, but she is not quite certain how and why, except that her boss is using her. The tone is resigned, but the speaker hangs in there, fighting. The song speaks to the goals and frustrations of many working women, and Parton, for all her huge fortune and great fame, is accepted into the sorority of working women.

Owing in part to exposure from the movie (in which Parton starred), this song became a great success, crossing over to the pop charts as well, and cementing Parton's appeal to non-country fans.

But You Know I Love You

"But You Know I Love You" describes another failed love affair, this one broken off by the speaker. The speaker wakes up from a dream of her lover and recalls her circumstances. She is on the road and has left behind many broken dreams. She wishes that love was enough to live on, but it is not. The life of the wanderer is the only life she knows and it's the only way she can make a living. She longs for a simpler time when problems were easy to solve. If only this problem were easy to solve, she would go running back to her lover. Nonetheless, even though circumstances keep them apart, she reminds him that she loves him.

The song is unusual, for rarely does the female protagonist of a song have the "wandering" gene. Further, it is unusual for a woman to give up a love relationship because she wants to continue with her work. Here, the necessity of work for a woman is not questioned. Only the fact that it prevents two lovers from being together is lamented, but when the choice is stated—work or relationship—the speaker has chosen work.

Though the song has some elements of story, it is mostly a lyric song aimed at capturing an emotion of sadness. The speaker has left her lover because circumstances have forced her to. Though she feels some regret, she does not know how she could have managed it differently. The world itself, she thinks, would have to be different, and she would have to be in a simpler time for the situation to resolve itself in a satisfying manner. In this sense, the song is reminiscent of Kristofferson's "Me And Bobby

McGee," because the speaker simply cannot provide what the lost love needs. In this song, the question of giving up her work never arises; it is simply her work and she must do it.

This is one of many hits that Parton has had as a solo act. It is notable, for it captures the sense of work as something men and women have to do, which may interfere with love relationships, but that cannot be helped. The issue of gender is not an issue; Parton assumes that it is the same for women as for men.

Here You Come Again

In "Here You Come Again," the speaker's lover returns after having left her. Instead of rejoicing at her great good fortune, she is actually quite rueful about the situation. Any pleasure she has at his return is mitigated by the circumstances; he returns just as she has created an independent life for herself, and though she values that life, she knows herself well enough to realize that she will allow him to return to her life and she will give up the strides she has made.

The idea of lovers continually leaving and then returning to each other even though the relationship is not satisfactory is not a new idea; Charley Pride's "When I Stop Leaving I'll Be Gone" is a case in point. But this takes a slightly different approach, showing how the speaker has just gotten her life together and has begun to get along without him. Therefore, his return is met with more regret than anything else. Yet the speaker is also slightly disgusted with herself, for she knows that she will abandon this new life she has constructed for the old life she had with him.

This song could, in fact, be seen as the mirror image or the flip side of the Charley Pride song, for now is it a woman who is left behind. Parton shows the situation from the woman's perspective. Like Pride's speaker, this one is disgusted with herself, for she knows what she will do. There is no suggestion that she could do otherwise; she doesn't even consider the option for herself, so intoxicating does she usually find his charms.

This song was another great hit for Parton. The tone, at once beleaguered, rueful and accepting, tests Parton's range, and she passes the test admirably.

I Will Always Love You

"I Will Always Love You" was written by Parton for Porter Wagoner after their breakup. The speaker says that if she stays, she will only get in the man's way. Therefore, she must leave. But, she says, she will always love him and will think of him with each step she takes on the new path she has chosen. Memories of him are all that she will take with her and she reminds him that she is not what he needs.

On a literal level, the song can be taken to mean that a woman is leaving her lover, because the relationship is not working, and she is only getting in the way of her lover.

Since Parton wrote it for her ex-partner—and since their breakup was acrimonious—it serves as an apology, an explanation and a recognition. The song also works to conflate real with imagined or alleged relationships. That is, many people suspected that Parton and Wagoner were lovers (which both coyly denied). What is more worthy of speculation than a love song written for a man with whom one never had a love affair?

Because the song can work on a number of different levels, it can be interpreted in a number of different ways. On one level, Parton intends it as a farewell song to an old partner. But it can also be seen as a breakup song in which a lover leaves, for the love relationship is no longer working. If both possibilities are accepted, others must be as well. The song could work equally well when a child leaves the nest, or even when an individual is preparing for death. Indeed, it has been taken in all these ways, such is the variety of its meanings. In general, it can be accepted as a farewell song, though who is saying farewell to whom varies.

Another big hit for Parton, this worked as a catharsis for her, and helped her resolve her relationship with Porter Wagoner. For thousands of listeners, it has been adapted to fulfill their needs, which is certainly one measure of a song's success.

Parton is concerned with women's roles. Like Lynn, she presents issues from the woman's point of view. Like Lynn, she also openly discusses sexuality, though in a slightly different way. She has serious and mocking songs about women's concerns (one of her mocking songs is called "P.M.S. Blues") but she readily takes the side of women and attempts to understand and answer their needs.

Suzy Bogguss

Suzy Bogguss once told *Music City News* that the best piece of advice she ever received was "don't underestimate your true goal and falsely pursue lesser ones. John Denny, a music publisher in Nashville, told me this when I first moved to town."[136] Since graduating from college, she has been wholeheartedly pursuing her true goal of becoming a well-known country music performer.

Born in 1956 in Aleda, Illinois, her childhood was unremarkable. Her parents both worked, so she was, as she puts it, a "latchkey kid." She learned to play the guitar as a teenager and later majored in art at Illinois State University, thinking that with a degree in metalsmithing she would create and sell jewelry for a living. But instead she toured as a country music singer for several years after college. Bogguss says she started booking herself by calling clubs and promoting herself as "just another chick singer."[137]

Eventually she arrived in Nashville. Probably the only country music performer with a cat named Chaucer, she made the rounds in Nashville, trying to drum up a job, a recording contract, anything. By 1988, she had received the Academy of Country

Music's Top New Female Vocalist award. She discovered what people want—to be sung to genuinely.

She calls Emmylou Harris an important influence. She also says Linda Ronstadt influenced her, as did folk music. Of her early career, she says, "one night I'd be playing in a really well-known folk club where everybody was sipping amaretto coffee, and the next night I'd be in a honky tonk where they were sitting on the floor."[138] She has always co-produced her music, booked her own shows and so on. This control is important to her, especially in an industry that tends to be difficult for women to enter and to compete in.

Like Mary Chapin Carpenter, Bogguss is a college-educated middle class performer who has been influenced by a wide variety of singers and musical styles. She, too, blends country with folk to produce a new sound, though she sings in the tradition of other independent female country music performers. Her troubadour nature resembles Harris', but she, too, is forging a distinctive style and voice of her own.

On the CD liner notes to "Something Up My Sleeve," she says, "Hey, I know there's a lot of great music out there today, so thanks for taking mine with you. There's also a lot of really good things to fight for in the world—pick some . . . it makes you feel wonderful."

Diamonds and Tears

"Diamonds and Tears" describes how the speaker looked for happiness with a lover, but what she got instead was self-knowledge. Even though she has loved and lost along the way, she has found something more important than that, though the suggestion is that the lovers may have had something to do with her enlightenment.

The speaker turns a cliché on its head; she'd cross burning bridges not to get to a lover, but to keep what she has learned. The song is unusual in that it emphasizes experience and knowledge over love and relationships. These last come and go, but experience and knowledge one gets to keep forever.

The song uses the symbols of diamonds and tears to show what matters in life; both diamonds and tears, we come to understand, are valuable. Both diamonds and tears have several meanings. Diamonds, of course, are valuable as a material commodity. They are also valuable because they stand for love and promises made. Tears, on the other hand, have no real value as a commodity, but they are without price as a symbol of the lessons one learns and the heartaches one encounters, which lead to greater understanding of the self.

The song is not important so much because it was a hit song (it wasn't) but because it gives an indication of Bogguss' concerns. She is more interested in self-discovery and self-expression than with love relationships.

"Hey, Cinderella" tackles the disillusionment women feel when their lives and marriages don't turn out as they have been led to expect. The speaker speaks for a group of female friends who believed in fairy tales and princes and played with Barbie dolls. They celebrated at each others' weddings, dancing and drinking champagne, but now, years later, they ask each other, do you ever want to ask Cinderella what the story is about? Perhaps we missed a page or two. The speaker says she wants to ask Cinderella, "does the shoe fit you now?"

The song is a masterful discussion of the disillusionment adult life brings. Raised with fantasies and fairy tales—and "Cinderella" is only one of these—children are never prepared for the real world. "Cinderella" stands for all the things that didn't work out as they should have—the hard work that is not rewarded, the husbands who are well-loved but still unfaithful, the children who are devotedly tended to and still turn out wrong—all these are mourned with the symbol of Cinderella. These women didn't get to go to the ball, after all.

It is only long after the wedding celebration that the women begin to wonder if perhaps the celebration wasn't premature. The speaker realizes that all the things that are celebrated in women's lives have little to do with their own accomplishments, and are events predicated on luck and fortune. She points out that what young women are prepared for is nothing like what they will face, so no wonder they feel confused, as if they have missed something.

This was a big hit for Bogguss, and its slightly unusual perspective was appreciated by female country music fans. It also showed that a song that stretched the boundaries of country music could be embraced by the country music culture.

Souvenirs

"Souvenirs" describes how the speaker, like Kerouac, set out to travel across the country, learning about the "real" America. But she wonders what happened to the waves of grain; all she sees are billboards from sea to shining sea. The speaker points out that all there "is" is souvenirs. Mt. Rushmore comes on a cup. The speaker even relates this to love. The "souvenir" experience has made everything seem unreal. She returns her lover's "dimestore" ring which turns her finger green, and which she calls a souvenir.

The contrast of ideas expressed in the song "America the Beautiful" with reality at the end of the twentieth century is uncomfortable. The song even makes us question the veracity of writings like Kerouac's, which celebrate something that no longer exists. The speaker says that no longer does one go anywhere for the experience, but instead one travels to collect souvenirs which identify the experience. One doesn't carry the experience in one's heart, but rather in one's suitcase, in the guise of some tacky memento. When the speaker returns her lover's ring, it is as if she is returning the souvenir that marks his affection for her; the ring is no longer a symbol of love, but a souvenir of it.

The song laments a sort of lost America. It is possible that the images of America that the speaker has were never real images, but she is upset with how much reality differs from her expectations. By the same token, the song laments a sort of lost youth for the speaker. Again, the images she has of herself and her life may never have reflected reality, but she is upset with how much reality differs from her expectations. This is evident in her breaking off the love relationship. The trip, which has shown her that all there is is souvenirs makes her question the reality of everything. Her distaste for the souvenirs prompts her to break off the relationship which is not genuine, either.

Though this song was never a big hit for Bogguss, it shows her skill with imagery and subtle analogy, and reveals some of her preoccupations with appearance versus reality, with expectations versus actuality.

You Wouldn't Say That To A Stranger

"You Wouldn't Say That To A Stranger" focuses on a troubled relationship. The two hurt each other and endanger their love; they mindlessly insult each other by saying things they wouldn't dream of saying to a stranger. The speaker wants them to pretend that they just met, because if they do so, if they meet as strangers, they won't say the things to each other that they wouldn't say to a stranger.

The song explores a timeless concern people have; how can people who say they love each other treat each other so unkindly? People are kinder and more polite to absolute strangers, who mean nothing to them, who probably will never be seen again, than they are to those they love. The simple, direct "you wouldn't say that to a stranger" reminds us of our obligations to each other, obligations we rarely meet.

The song urges us to remember that even if we love one another, we must treat each other carefully. If we do not, we run the risk of saying or doing something that cannot be forgiven. Instead of discovering what those unforgivable words and actions are, it is best to avoid the possibility of doing or saying them

The song demonstrates that Bogguss has traditional concerns as well as non-traditional ones. In this case, the concern is with a love relationship that is under stress. Here, she presents a philosophy of love that reminds both her and her lover of their responsibilities to each another.

Suzy Bogguss is one of the current generation of female country music performers who place an emphasis on discussing issues of particular concern to women. In addition, she sings about the theme of love from traditional as well as non-traditional perspectives. Her wide variety of musical influences and her atypical (for country music) upbringing and education all permeate her songs.

❀   ❀

Songs of Life

These singers tackle women's issues in various ways. They express alternative points of view or show non-traditional images of women. Even their more traditional songs are presented from the woman's point of view. In short, they respect and celebrate the concerns that are closest to women's hearts. These singers have also attempted to open doors for other women and to help them succeed in the country music business as well.

Political and Social Issues

Country music has always been considered conservative, both with respect to politics and to religion. In fact, travel writer Arthur Frommer blasts the entire town of Branson, Missouri, for its "quasi-political, quasi-religious" entertainment. "Patriotism for profit" and "religion for profit" are its attributes, he says, calling it "the capital of the religious right." Some entertainers use their theaters for "intensely political, extremely right-wing viewpoints."[139] It is true that when politics are mentioned, country music performers usually stand right of center. Yet political or social statements are not always well-accepted by country music culture. "Independence Day," a song by Gretchen Peters, sung by Martina McBride, is about domestic violence and has a violent ending. On stage, the song ends with fireworks. For this reason, several large radio stations refused to play it—at least until the O.J. Simpson murder trial brought attention to the problem of domestic violence.

Country music has a tradition of protest and anti-establishment music. Country music performers comment upon political and social issues frequently, sometimes with novelty recordings like "Saddam Hussein Still Has a Job But I Don't." More often, they sing thoughtful songs that question the status quo or unthinking acceptance of certain norms.

However, Steve Terrell, a columnist for the *Santa Fe New Mexican* lists several country music songs in his "Top 10 Right-Wing Songs," including Merle Haggard's "Okie from Muskogee," and "The Fighting Side of Me," as well as "In America" by Charlie Daniels; he also includes Hank Williams, Jr.'s "A Country Boy Can Survive."

While these political songs are in some sense reactionary, other political songs such as Johnny Cash's "The One On The Right Is On The Left" take a more sophisticated and humorous approach. Social issues are also relevant to country music singers, and these include concerns such as domestic violence and child abuse. Indeed, growing awareness among performers about the dangers of substance abuse has led to fewer songs celebrating alcohol and drunkenness, and more songs advocating a different approach to handling problems. Many singing careers have ended with alcohol problems and performers today are more likely to go to the Betty Ford Treatment Center than to simply live with the problem or sing about it. In fact, several successful songs, such as Neil McCoy's "If I Was A Drinking Man," discuss how the speaker has become a sober person, now that he or she has realized the problems drinking has caused.

Of the country music performers who have sung about political and social issues, three are prominent. They are Johnny Cash, his daughter Rosanne Cash, and the extremely successful Garth Brooks.

Johnny Cash

Like other country music performers, Johnny Cash started on the conservative side. His songs, like "Ragged Old Flag," extolled a sort of unexamined patriotism, but his lyrics became more complex and he became more influential in folk music, especially after his collaboration with Bob Dylan.

Born in Arkansas in 1932, the son of a sharecropper, Cash himself worked in the cotton fields during his youth. His brother Jack, a religious young man, was killed in a work-related accident, an event that has haunted Cash all his life.

As an adult, Cash has battled drug and alcohol addictions frequently. He got religion in the mid 1970s, but he still broadened his political beliefs. His prison concerts, social commentaries, and work songs have all produced a more mainstream, populist political person. "Bitter Tears," which protested treatment of Native Americans, was controversial on its release in 1964, but Cash never shied away from controversy.

Cash, who was inducted into the Hall of Fame in 1980, appeals to both pop and hardcore country fans. His appeal is timeless and he is as versatile as he is enduring. He began his career being groomed as an heir to Elvis Presley, but from that rockabilly beginning, he has moved to protest albums, folk, and rock. The Man in Black with his outlaw image is a clean, religious family man these days. Johnny Cash, known as John to his friends and industry insiders, has recently become interested in heavy metal because "you can feel the music, not just hear it." He admires the lighting and special effects of such shows. It also has given him an appreciation, such as his daughter Rosanne has, for people's right to say what they think. He considers it "presumptuous" for people his age to think they're finally doing something to raise their children right by censoring music. Johnny's openness to these various influences has helped him stay on the charts for thirty years. He has been rediscovered by a younger audience, who like to hear his pre-1970s rockabilly music.

He has sold more than fifty million records and for over thirty years in a row placed two singles a year on the country music charts. He has sung on almost 500 albums. Now involved with the group called The Highwaymen, Cash is touring more frequently than in the past.

Cash is appreciated for his touch with country music. For him, "like all superior country artists . . . the story is everything. His writing is spare, detailed and straightforward. . . . He can conjure any emotion."[140] Plain spoken poetry, it has been called.

Two generations of country music stars appeared at this Waterloo, Iowa concert in 1974.

His truisms are the kind generations of children have learned. He talks about pollution, he talks about songs that make a difference. He became popular because his work deals with the unpopular, uncomfortable truths of life,[141] and his audience could identify with him. If they work hard, well, the King of Country's deep voice sounds like hard work.

Man In Black

"Man In Black" describes why Cash dresses in black, in answer to the question people ask him most often. He says there is a reason for his somber appearance. He wears black for the poor and hungry, for the prisoners who have paid for their crimes, for those who haven't heard the word of God, and others, too. He says he will try to carry some of the darkness off with him and he will wear black until the world is in better shape and he can wear colors. He says he would like to wear a rainbow of colors but he is obligated to be the Man in Black.

Cash creates his own myth or legend here; he wore black long before he wrote the song, and he admits in his autobiography that he doesn't even know the reason why he started. People frequently asked him and he decided to make a statement. Still, it makes a good reason and a believable myth, one that his audience will accept.

Even though Cash did not set out to deliberately wear black as a message to others, the black he wears has been transformed into a statement, one of his own choosing. The song describes the political and social beliefs of Cash. He is sympathetic to the poor and the downtrodden, and to the prisoners who have paid for their crimes, or are being held for political reasons, and so on. The song works as a position paper, only easier to understand.

The song was popular. Although not a huge hit, it confirmed for many people what they thought Johnny Cash represented. Once he had stated his beliefs in no uncertain terms, listeners could feel assured that if they bought his music and attended his performances, they would be supporting a position they could accept as well. For the country music audience, it is important that performers take a stand on political and social issues, and here Cash supplies them with his stand on a variety of issues.

The One On The Right Is On The Left

"The One on the Right Is on The Left" is an upbeat, comic song about politics. The speaker describes a musical folk group that sings mountain ballads. They are very talented but they suffer from political incompatibility. The one on the right is on the left, and vice versa; the one in the rear is a Methodist. The song describes the trials and tribulations of this politically incompatible group, which ends in a free-for-all.

The speaker comments that you can't mix politics and folk songs—which of course you can, as the speaker well knows. The song cleverly pillories the political orientation of many folk groups; instead of singing, they become so involved in politics that they become useless as singers. But the song itself is a joyous political statement. It wryly uses tortured syntax and long, seldom-used words to make its point.

The tortured lyrics and awkward melody defeat the whole purpose of saying that singers should just sing; the song deconstructs or falls apart like the group whose adventures it recounts. That is, the song is neither melodious nor soundly constructed. It is not any of the things usually demanded in a song, so it is not even successful as a song. It is successful merely as a statement, doing exactly the same thing its speaker criticizes others for doing. The song pokes fun at others, but also makes fun of itself as well.

The song is a catchy, fun tune and it reinforces the audience's idea of Cash as a wry commentator on the human condition. He does the very thing that he criticizes in others, and he knows it, so he does it with a sense of humor and expects us to take it with a grain of salt.

Folsom Prison Blues

In "Folsom Prison Blues," the speaker, an inmate, hears a train, a lonesome sound. He is stuck in prison and hasn't seen the sun in ages. He wonders what others are doing on the train. Other people keep on moving, and that drives him crazy. If he were free, he would get as far away from Folsom Prison as he could.

The song has the memorable line "I shot a man in Reno just to watch him die." The speaker is a bit out of character for Cash, who while he might sing of people considered outlaws and wanderers, nonetheless sings about people who are fundamentally good and decent. The speaker here expresses no remorse for his actions; indeed, he expresses no emotion other than the wish to be free.

"Folsom Prison Blues" is probably the archetype for all prison songs, though others explore aspects of prison life. Haggard sang about prison, but he had actually been an inmate. Cash himself never experienced prison life the way the prisoners he sings about have. The song deals with a past issue, one that no longer preoccupies country music performers. The symbols of the train and the prison stand for the aloneness and wandering that make an outlaw an outlaw.

This is probably Cash's most famous song, and it is his signature song, even though he is not the kind of person who would shoot a man just to watch him die. The song acts as a catharsis for the audience, as it celebrates images of the outlaw and the wanderer.

A Boy Named Sue

"A Boy Named Sue" is the story of a boy who grows up without a father. Before the father leaves, he names his son "Sue." The son gets into many fights and grows up quickly. He becomes a wanderer, so ashamed is he of his name, and he vows to kill the man who named him. Eventually, he finds that "dirty mangy dog" who is his father. He hits his father hard, his father hits back, and they have a fistfight. When the dust settles, the son has the upper hand and the father explains. He knew his son would grow up fatherless and it would be hard, so he gave his son this name to make him become strong. The son decides not to kill his father and they are reconciled, calling each other "son" and "pa." The son realizes that his father was trying to do what was best and says if he ever has a son—he'll name him Bill or Joe, anything but Sue.

This is another comic song, in which Cash subverts our expectations. The song has all the elements of a traditional revenge song, but it is a demented revenge song, because after all, the only crime is an inappropriate name. But then, we see how it has affected all aspects of the speaker's life, forcing him to become a loner. But that in itself is comic, for we are not accustomed to hearing the tale of an outcast who is a loner just because of his name. The self-realization at the end is also comic—we expect the speaker to decide to name his son Sue, too.

The song keeps setting up our expectations and then mocking them. By thwarting our expectations the song pokes fun at those expectations, as well as at traditional songs and typical country music messages. At the same time, the song relies on those messages and songs to set up the expectations that it denies.

Johnny Cash is a legendary performer, one who did not and does not shy away from controversy. Like Loretta Lynn, he is always willing to speak his mind, and he does so on a variety of political and social issues. He always keeps his sense of humor about him, however, and never takes himself too seriously, despite his image of the serious, stark Man in Black.

Rosanne Cash

Rosanne Cash, daughter of Johnny Cash, has made her own mark on the country music scene. Born in Memphis in 1955, to Vivian Liberton and Johnny Cash, who divorced when she was eleven, she later became a rebellious teenager heavily into drugs. She joined her father on the road in 1973, when she graduated from high school. By the early eighties, she was singing on her own.

By 1981, Cash was considered a major creative country music singer. Of course, as a descendant of the Cash family, influenced by Cash's wife, June Carter, country music was expected of Rosanne Cash. In drug treatment by 1984, she wrote about her pain, recovery, strength and other personal and intimate experiences. By 1985, Cash had beaten cocaine, rescued a faltering marriage, and borne three daughters. She wrote many songs on her *Rhythm and Romance* album, which ranges from country to rock and was dubbed "yuppie music." She was referred to as a member of the "New Nashville," singers who were breaking down differences between rock, pop, folk and country.

Unlike most country music stars, though, she was not certain she wanted to be close to her fans or even part of the country music culture/community. Some of her songs, like "Oh Yes I Can" are frankly feminist, while others deal with abuse and other social problems.

By 1990, however, with the conservatism of Nashville grating on her nerves, she recorded the album *Interiors,* which was not considered country enough to be played by country music radio programmers. In *Interiors,* she sang about child abuse and substance abuse, plus infidelity and other relationship problems, themes which have served other country music performers well. Clearly, though, since Cash has chosen to distance herself from the country music culture, the industry has chosen to distance itself from her.

Now living in New York City, she maintains a Nashville apartment and is sorting out her musical direction. While Cash sings love songs, she refuses to buy into the "defenseless-female mentality" that she thinks permeates mainstream country music. Her approach is down to earth and honest. Her candor makes her music a bit more cynical than that of many love songs, but she is considered witty and genuine. As one music critic sums it up, "country music's sentimentality has always been a part of its charm, but the hokey extremes have often alienated young urban listeners. Other unattractive aspects—the right-wing divisiveness—simply don't apply anymore."[142]

"Country music offers a clarity of feelings," Cash said in 1988, "but sometimes it can be hard to define because it's constantly being redefined."[143] Of her songwriting she says, "I listen to a lot of music, but I listen to people, not trends."[144]

As an environmentalist, Cash is concerned with providing her listeners with information; she calls her concern an extension of motherhood. She also garnered attention for her support of 2 Live Crew, Guns 'N Roses, and comedian Andrew Dice Clay, who have been criticized for obscenity. She opposes record labelling and though she won't allow her children to listen to some entertainers, she defends the performers' right to say what they want. "The issue isn't morality," she says, "the issue is government intervention. There's a lot of garbage in the world that I don't want my children exposed to . . . but that's a function of parenting."[145]

Like other country music families, the Cash family has had more than one generation involved in the business. Johnny Cash married June Carter, from the famous Carter Family. She herself established a singing career and, when she married Johnny, began singing duets with him. Cash credited the Carter family with helping him to recover his sobriety and to appreciate country music. His association with a famous country music family influenced him; it also influenced his daughter Rosanne. Other famous country music families include father and daughter Mel and Pam Tillis, and the two Hank Williamses as well as the mother and daughter group, The Judds.

Cash's recording *King's Record Shop* contains her most country songs. These deal with a wide variety of themes, issues and concerns.

RunAway Train

"RunAway Train" compares passionate love to a runaway train. In this case, the speaker and her lover have ignored warnings, as a conductor might not see signals because of the rain. They can't stop now—even trying to stop would be as futile as waving a lantern to stop a runaway train. The speaker says ruefully that she has done this before, so therefore, she knows how it will all end and she knows that they will pay a price for their love.

The comparison with a train is fascinating. The train as a symbol in country music can stand for freedom, wandering, loneliness and adventure (these ideas are connected), but this song capitalizes on the idea of the train being dangerously out of control—in which case it cannot mean any of these things. It is a vivid image of passions being uncontrolled. The images of warning lights flashing and lanterns being swung are reminders of the more subtle warnings the lovers must have had. The various images associated with the runaway train clarify the emotions and the situation of the lovers here.

The idea that sometimes love and passion can be uncontrollable and therefore dangerous is an old theme, and one that country music has dealt with before. The nature of such emotions—beyond control—is of interest to many observers of human nature. In this song, why their love is so dangerous is unclear. Perhaps it is illegitimate in some way, or perhaps it is so passionate that it will eventually burn itself out. Perhaps the two are sacrificing other things in their lives to participate in the love affair that will necessarily end by the nature of its intensity.

This is one of Cash's better known songs, and it updates the symbol of the train. By combining the idea of the train with a theme of love, the song becomes something of a social statement, for it is in society's best interest to control both runaway trains and runaway passions.

I Don't Have To Crawl

In "I Don't Have To Crawl," the speaker points out that her lover pretends that he doesn't know her. She says she could leave him alone if she tried. She asserts that she could be long gone if she wanted to. She can just walk away; she doesn't have to wait on him; she doesn't have to crawl.

The speaker here adds a note of defiance to the usual been done wrong song. Though we do not know what exactly the lover has done to make the speaker so unhappy, we know that she has reached a state of decision. She realizes she doesn't have to behave the way she has been behaving. But she hasn't been moved to action yet.

The rebellious tone suggests that the speaker will act, but the slow, painful melody suggest that it will be a while before the speaker is finally moved to act.

Instead of merely bemoaning her fate, the speaker here is aware that she has a choice. She doesn't have to crawl or behave in anything less than a perfectly dignified manner. She doesn't have to accept anything less than what she wants. If she chooses to accept less or to crawl, that is her own choice and her own responsibility. The song focuses on the idea of choice and responsibility, not only as it applies to this particular relationship, but to other areas of life as well.

Though this was not a big hit for Rosanne Cash, it typifies many of her concerns. Cash sings about love and relationships. When she does, she is interested in that moment of choice, and in the power that choice confers on an individual, regardless of what course of action the individual eventually chooses.

Rosie Strike Back

"Rosie Strike Back" is about a battered woman whom the speaker exhorts to "strike back" not through any physical means, but through leaving, taking only the baby and the clothes she is wearing. The speaker tells the woman that "he" won't change and that he will always take it out on her. The narrator pleads with the woman—don't be a victim.

Such social awareness and social commentary is not unusual for country music, though generally it is not perceived as being socially aware and responsive. This song helps to illustrate the point that country music is about the real world, even when it is a not very attractive real world.

More than anything, the song is a simple call to action. The speaker wants Rosie—and the rest of us—to recognize that abuse does not have to be tolerated and that to stop it, the victim must leave, must refuse to be a victim. Beyond that, however, the song does not offer any solutions. It is merely a reflection of a social reality and a response to it.

The song's importance stems from the way it tackles the issue of domestic violence. As one of the earliest country music songs to address this issue, it is significant as a response to growing awareness of spousal abuse.

The Way We Make A Broken Heart

"The Way We Make A Broken Heart" acts like a recipe or a how-to song for hurting another person. The speaker is evidently addressing her male lover. She assures him that he will get used to telling lies. Lesson #1 consists of learning to hurt his wife. In lesson #2, the wife longs for him when he is not there. In lesson #3, she'll beg him to stop what he's doing. In lesson #4, he will leave her. And, while the wife may find someone else, she probably will be hurt again. The lessons all add up to a broken heart.

The song sets up an interesting dualism. The speaker is a detached observer who is also somehow engaged, for she expresses a certain remorse, a certain distaste for her role, that of mentor instructing the man who is the student. The speaker might be the man's lover, or a commentator, or even an aspect of fate.

Though the man is being taught how to make a broken heart, it is his wife who learns the lessons. She is the one who is hurt, who longs for him, who begs him to stay. She is the instrument through which the whole program is taught; if she completes each lesson correctly, the man will have learned how to make a broken heart.

Rosanne Cash is significant to country music, for her contributions during her brief country music career showed the possibilities inherent in country music. She is interested in social and political issues and tackles them in her songs. She is also capable of singing traditional love songs and has even sung several of her father's songs, but she is most important for the voice of political and social commentary which she has added.

Garth Brooks

Garth Brooks is perhaps the most successful of all country music performers ever. His mega stardom has allowed him to say what he thinks. He has sung about hungry children, homosexuality, the environment, date rape, and civil rights and has sold 50 million albums in the US alone while doing so.

Born February 7, 1962 in Tulsa, Oklahoma, the last of six children, he got a banjo for his 16th birthday. He attended Oklahoma State University on an athletic scholarship and studied journalism. He worked as a bouncer, which is how he met his wife (she was in a fight with another female patron). The story sounds almost apocryphal: he listened to George Strait in 1981 and decided to become a country music singer; he moved to Nashville in 1987; from there, he achieved his legendary stardom.

Brooks is pictured as a sensitive, family-oriented man, by his fans and by the media. His problems (infidelity, career questions) are not alien to his fans. He is considered an honest, straightforward individual, addressing serious issues which he himself has faced. On the cover of his most recent album, a collection of his hits, Brooks poses wrapped in an American flag, emphasizing his patriotism and traditionalism which may not be apparent in his songs.

He has been criticized for creating hard rock-like spectacles, but he has certainly made country music interesting. His showmanship is different from what many country music performers do and, like Elvis Presley, his music is an acquired taste. In fact, he could be considered the heir to Presley.

His wife has resented his tell-all lyrics. His "cleverly contemporary songs" are backed by a traditional sounding band.[146] "I don't mind relating my feelings," Garth says, "And I like to think my lyrics can appeal to and be understood by everyone from yuppies to truck drivers." He says, "country music isn't 'my dad got run over at the truck stop right after my wife left me this morning.' The music is set in a manner that everybody can relate to, not just the guy driving the truck."[147]

The influence country music has on other lives cannot be overestimated, he thinks. He received a letter from a woman who said she was considering suicide until she heard "If Tomorrow Never Comes" and studied its message.

As a performer he kisses the women and shakes hands with the men. Like other country music performers, Garth says, "there's millions of people in this town that are ten times more talented than I am. It's just getting your break."[148]

He has a reputation for signing autographs for hours after a concert. Called "pleasantly modest and unassuming," he is amazed at his success. Garth enjoys people whether they are fans or not. Recently he wrote a column for a magazine describing how he feels about his work so far. But, he says, "this isn't about selling product. It's about communicating between an artist and the people," and he thanks his fans.[149]

The Dance

"The Dance" describes the learning process the speaker goes through when his lover leaves him. He says he is glad he didn't know what would happen, because he would have skipped the relationship, and thereby missed "the dance"—that is, the pleasure of living and loving. While he might have missed the pain, he would have missed out on the experience, which was valuable.

Garth Brooks calls this his "career song" and he says when he first heard the song, "I felt like jumping out of my skin and standing on the table and screaming to everyone in the room, 'did you hear what I just heard?'"[150]

The song details a "living" theme in the sense that its message is about how to live one's life to the fullest. Living well does not mean avoiding all heartache and pain, but enjoying and participating in living. The wonderful moments of joy, Brooks points out, cannot exist without the contrast of the moments of pain. This philosophy is expressed in other Brooks songs as well.

As a career song, this captures the essence of Brooks' philosophy of life. As a huge success, it clearly touched the hearts of many fans, who accepted the philosophy it represents.

We Shall Be Free

"We Shall Be Free" shares the philosophy of the speaker, who is just an ordinary guy. He describes his vision of a world in which all people are free, and everyone is kind to one another. He envisions shelter for the poor and protection for those who speak out, and he looks for a clean sky and ocean. With all of these things together, "we shall be free."

Brooks says about this, "[It] is definitely and easily the most controversial song I have ever done. . . . I never thought there would be any problems with this song. . . . All I can say about 'We Shall Be Free' is that I will stand by every line of this song as long as I live."

The song points out that as long as anyone is oppressed, we are all oppressed. Brooks says that we are all still in bondage, and not just because of what we do to each other, but because of how we treat our natural surroundings. Until we can learn, understand and take care of everything that is our responsibility, we will be unhappy, and imprisoned. This point of view is exactly the same point of view expressed by civil rights activists, and, though refreshing, is not unusual in country music.

As both a controversial song and a huge hit for Brooks, this song is known to many different audiences. While Brooks was surprised at the controversy it generated, he was pleased to stand for these values. Because of his legendary status, he is more able to tackle political and social issues and have people listen to him, instead of merely criticize.

The Thunder Rolls

"The Thunder Rolls" was another controversial song for Brooks, not so much for its content, but for the video that accompanied it. In the song, a woman waits for her husband to get home. A storm brews as she waits, and she thinks it might be the cause of his delay. When he does arrive home, he smells of perfume and alcohol. The husband knows his wife knows he was unfaithful, and he isn't sure what to do. The song leaves the situation unresolved. In the video, however, it is clear that the song is about spousal abuse, which adds another layer of tension and meaning to the lyrics. The video was banned by various television stations because of the violence it depicted (the wife kills the husband), but Brooks' stature as a country music performer persuaded other station managers to run the video.

Brooks says, cryptically, "There is no doubt this is the toughest song . . . only music could withstand what this song has gone through." He is referring to the controversy generated by this song, which he was also able to withstand.

In the song, the tensions rise as the storm brews. The storm breaks as the erring husband arrives home. This natural thunderstorm is a counterpoint to the emotional storm which will happen between the two people and serves to foreshadow the events that will follow. Just as the storm is wild and uncontrollable, so, too, does the situation become wild and uncontrollable.

This was another hit for Brooks, though it generated much controversy. Brooks does not allow such debates to influence his work. He, like Loretta Lynn, says what he thinks and insists that others be allowed to listen to it if they want.

In "Friends in Low Places," the speaker's former lover is getting married, and he shows up at the reception, a black tie affair, in his cowboy boots. The contrast between the two could not be greater; the country and the city are in conflict. It is clear that the speaker thinks that his former lover has given up something real and honest for material things. The speaker accuses her of living in an ivory tower, but he says he won't complain. He is going to rely on his friends "in low places" to cheer him up.

Brooks says that he sang the song on a demo tape early in his career "and for the next two weeks the chorus of this song kept running through my head." He made the decision to record it sometime—a decision that has proven wise.

Although the song is in some respects simply about a scorned lover who turns to drinking and carousing to numb his pain and cheer himself up, it has a subtext of class issues. Clearly, the woman decided he wasn't good enough for her, which causes resentment not only in the speaker but in the speaker's friends and also in the listeners. The country boy and the city girl have come together in country music songs in the past, but not this time. The speaker suggests that if she doesn't appreciate him, he knows people who do.

This is one of Brooks' most spectacular hits. It shows his ability to handle a traditional country music song, one that celebrates country music values. The speaker here clearly understands that it is his class that is at issue, and he makes fun of the whole idea of class, pointing out that a person's worth has more to do with what's inside than what is outside.

As his incredible success shows, Garth Brooks has managed to touch a collective country music nerve. While some of his songs are simply for fun, he is known as a performer who stands up for what he thinks is right. He is considered a decent, loving family man, and his slightly liberal values endear him to a newer, younger generation of fans.

❀

Singers who tackle issues of social and political concern find that they must temper their work with humor and rowdiness. They realize that they cannot be all serious all the time. Often, the performer will add love songs or living songs to his or her collection, so that it is not overweighted with too many songs about important issues. This would risk losing the attention of one's fans, if one only seemed to tackle serious, worldwide problems and not the specific details of everyday life. Still, performers take these global issues, and by making them personal, show how the issues affect all individuals.

Some Conclusions

As Kenny Rogers tells us in "The Gambler," you have to know when to hold 'em and when to fold 'em, and for this book, it's time to fold. This analysis of country music and country music lyrics is just a starting point. Others will have their own readings and their own interpretations of the music. One thing is clear, however: as long as there are heartaches, injustices and wars left to fight, there will be country music, for these are the very essence of country music. Melodies may change, become more complex and difficult; the vocals may become more polished and refined, but the examination of the human condition that characterizes country music will continue. As musical influences continue to expand, as different musical styles are explored, and as more and more young singers experiment with the music, the sound of country music will grow, but its fundamental nature will not change.

As its ever-increasing audience suggests, country music appeals to almost anyone interested in listening to the music of everyday experience, of everyday life. Since it first began achieving mass acceptance and popularity in the late forties and early fifties, country music has addressed issues and concerns that other musical styles have avoided. By tackling controversial subjects, and admitting to personal failures, country music singers and songwriters have achieved a unique rapport with their audience. The sincerity and authenticity of the performer and the performance is the basic measure of a song's success.

Though the melodies of country music are simple, the lyrics are not. They reflect the ambiguous, difficult terrain of human life and endeavor. As works of literature, as poetry, these songs are worthy of serious study in themselves, not merely as representations of folk culture or popular culture. Country music occupies itself with love, with living "right," with social and political issues, including gender roles. These are the themes and concerns of literature. Country music will long provide the arena for social and political dialogue and for the discussion of basic, timeless human concerns.

Song Bibliography

Suzy Bogguss

"Diamonds And Tears" (Matraca Berg/Gary Harrison) Warner-Tamerlane Publishing Corp., 1993.

"Hey Cinderella" (Suzy Bogguss/Matraca Berg/Gary Harrison) Famous Music Corp., 1993.

"Souvenirs" (Gretchen Peters) Sony Cross Keys Pub. Co., 1991.

"You Wouldn't Say That To A Stranger" (Pat Bunch/Doug Crider) August Wind Music, 1993.

Garth Brooks

"The Dance" (Tony Arata) MorganActive Songs Inc., 1990.

"Friends in Low Places" (Dewayne Blackwell/Earl Bud Lee) Music Ridge Music, Inc., 1991.

"The Thunder Rolls" (Pat Alger/Garth Brooks) Bait and Beer Music, 1991.

"We Shall Be Free" (Stephanie Davis/Garth Brooks) EMI Blackwood Music, 1992.

Mary Chapin Carpenter

"He Thinks He'll Keep Her" (Mary Chapin Carpenter/Don Schlitz) EMI April Music, 1992.

"I Feel Lucky" (Mary Chapin Carpenter/Don Schlitz) EMI April Music, 1992.

"The Hard Way" (Mary Chapin Carpenter) EMI April Music, 1992.

"Never Had It So Good" (Mary Chapin Carpenter/John Jennings) Getarealjob Music, 1988.

Johnny Cash

"A Boy Named Sue" (Shel Silverstein) BMI, 1969.

"Folsom Prison Blues" (John R. Cash) House of Cash, Inc., 1955.

"Man In Black" (John R. Cash) House of Cash, Inc., 1971.

"The One On The Right Is On The Left" (John R. Cash) House of Cash, Inc., 1966.

Rosanne Cash

"I Don't Have To Crawl" (Rodney Crowell) Columbia, 1987.

"Rosie Strike Back" (Eliza Gilkyson) Columbia, 1987.

"RunAway Train" (John Stewart) Columbia, 1987.

"The Way We Make A Broken Heart" (John Hiatt) Columbia, 1987.

Patsy Cline

"Crazy" (Willie Nelson) BMI, 1961.

"I Fall To Pieces" (Hank Cochran/Harlan Howard) BMI, 1960.

"She's Got You" (Hank Cochran) BMI, 1961.

"You Belong To Me" (Pee Wee King/Redd Stewart/Chilton Price) BMI, 1962.

Bob Dylan

"Girl From The North Country" (Bob Dylan) Warner Brothers, 1963.

"Lay, Lady, Lay" (Bob Dylan) Big Sky Music, 1969.

"Tell Me That It Isn't True" (Bob Dylan) Big Sky Music, 1969.

"Tonight I'll Be Staying Here With You" (Bob Dylan) Big Sky Music, 1969.

Merle Haggard

"I'm A Lonesome Fugitive" (Liz Anderson/Casey Anderson) Capitol, 1967.

"Mama Tried" (Merle Haggard) Capitol, 1968.

"Okie From Muskogee" (Merle Haggard/Roy Burris) Capitol, 1969.

"(My Friends Are Gonna Be) Strangers" (Liz Anderson) Capitol, 1965.

Emmylou Harris

"Boulder to Birmingham" (Emmmylou Harris/Bill Danoff) Wait & See Music, 1974.

"Making Believe" (Jimmy Work) Acuff-Rose Pub. Inc., 1976.

151

❋

**Songs
of Life**

"One of These Days" (Earl Montgomery) Altam Pub. Co., 1975.

"Two More Bottles of Wine" (Delbert McClinton) ABC Dunhill Music, Inc., 1976.

Kris Kristofferson

"Help Me Make It Through The Night" (Kris Kristofferson) Resaca Music, Inc., 1971.

"Me and Bobby McGee" (Kris Kristofferson) Resaca Music, Inc., 1971.

"Sunday Mornin' Comin' Down" (John R. Cash) House of Cash, Inc., 1971.

"Why Me?" (Kris Kristofferson) Resaca Music, Inc., 1972.

k. d. lang

"Black Coffee" (Peggy Lee) Sire Records, Shadowland, 1988.

"I'm Down to My Last Cigarette" (Harlan Howard) Sire Records, Shadowland, 1988.

"Shadowland" (Charles Tobias/Dick Hyman) Sire Records, Shadowland, 1988.

"Western Stars" (Chris Isaak) Sire Records, Shadowland, 1988.

Loretta Lynn

"Coal Miner's Daughter" (Loretta Lynn) Sure Fire Music Co. Inc, 1970.

"The Pill" (Lorene Allen/Don McHan/T.D. Bayless) Coal Miner's Music and Guaranty Music, Inc., 1973.

"Rated X" (Loretta Lynn) Sure Fire Music Co. Inc., 1971.

"When the Tingle Becomes A Chill" (Loretta Lynn) Coal Miner's Music, 1976.

Reba McEntire

"Have I Got A Deal For You" (Michael P. Henney/Jackson Leap) BMI, 1985.

"He Broke Your Memory Last Night" (Dickey Lee/Bucky Jones) BMI, 1984.

"Only In My Mind" (Reba McEntire) BMI, 1985.

"Somebody Should Leave" (Harlan Howard/Chick Rains) BMI, 1984.

Dolly Parton

"9 to 5" (Dolly Parton) BMI, 1980.

"But You Know I Love You" (Mike Settle) BMI, 1981.

"Here You Come Again" (Barry Mann/Cynthia Weil) BMI, 1977.

"I Will Always Love You" (Dolly Parton) BMI, 1974

Charley Pride

"Is Anybody Goin' To San Antone?" (Charley Pride) RCA, 1970.

"Oklahoma Morning" (Charley Pride) RCA, 1974.

"Tennessee Girl" (Charley Pride) RCA, 1975.

"When I Stop Leaving (I'll Be Gone)" (Charley Pride) RCA, 1978.

Kenny Rogers

"Daytime Friends" (Ben Peters) BMI, 1977.

"Lucille" (Waylon Jennings) BMI, 1977.

"Reuben James" (Mike Settle) BMI, 1969.

"Ruby, Don't Take Your Love to Town" (Mel Tillis) Cedarwood Publishing, Co., 1966.

Ernest Tubb

"Pass the Booze" (Ernest Tubb) Hill and Range Songs, Inc., 1964.

"Thanks A Lot" (Eddie Miller) Hill and Range Songs, Inc., 1963.

"Thirty Days" (Ernest Tubb) Hill and Range Songs, Inc., 1955.

"Walking the Floor Over You" (Ernest Tubb) Hill and Range Songs, Inc., 1943.

Tanya Tucker

"One Love At A Time" (David Malloy) BMI, 1986.

"Strong Enough To Bend" (David Malloy) BMI, 1989.

"What's Your Mama's Name, Child" (Dolores Fuller) 1973.

"Would You Lay With Me (In a Field of Stone)" (Dolores Fuller) BMI, 1973.

Hank Williams, Jr.

"The American Dream" (Hank Williams, Jr.) Bo Cephus Music Co., 1982

"A Country Boy Can Survive" (Hank Williams, Jr.) Bo Cephus Music Co., 1982.

"Dixie On My Mind" (Hank Williams, Jr.) Bo Cephus Music Co., 1981.

"Family Tradition" (Hank Williams, Jr.) Bo Cephus Music Co., 1979.

Hank Williams, Sr.

"Cold, Cold Heart" (Hank Williams) Fred Rose Music, Inc., 1951.

"I Ain't Got Nothing But Time" (Hank Williams) Fred Rose Music, Inc., 1951.

"Long Gone Lonesome Blues" (Hank Williams) Fred Rose Music, Inc., 1950.

"Lost Highway" (Leon Payne) Fred Rose Music, Inc., 1948.

Selected Reading

Allen, Bob. "Twenty Questions with Tim McGraw," *Country Music* (July 1995), 16-17.

Bowden, Betsy. *Performed Literature: Words and Music by Bob Dylan* (Bloomington, Indiana: Indiana University Press, 1982).

Bradley, S.A.J., trans. and ed. *Anglo-Saxon Poetry* (Rutland, Vermont: Charles E. Tuttle, Co., 1982).

Brinkhoff, Peg. "Cow Camp Chronicles," *Country America* (July/August 1995), 64-68.

[Brooks, Garth]. "Garth Brooks: In His Own Words," *Country Song Roundup* (October 1995), 5.

Brown, Charles T. *Music U.S.A.* (Englewood Cliffs, New Jersey: Prentice-Hall, 1986).

Bufwack, Mary A. and Robert K. Oermann. *Finding Her Voice* (New York: Crown Publishers, Inc., 1993).

Chandler, Arline. "Making Mountain Music," *Country America* (May 1995), 52-53.

Clark, Valerie. "Fan Clubs: What To Expect," *Cross Country* (June 1995), 14.

Cobb, James C. "Country Music and the 'Southernization' of America," in *All That Glitters,* ed. George H. Lewis (Bowling Green, Ohio: Bowling Green University Popular Press, 1993), 75-86.

"Country Beat," *Country America* (July 1995), 118.

Dougherty, Steve and Marge Sellinger. "Urbane Cowgirl Blues," *People* (August 31, 1992).

Ehlert, Bob. "Readin' and Writin' Country Music," *Country America* (July 1995), 77-78.

Ellison, Curtis W. *Country Music Culture* (Jackson, Mississippi: University Press of Mississippi, 1995).

Flans, Robyn. "Corporate Country: Who's Sponsoring the Hot Summer Tours?" *Country Fever* (August 1995), 26-30.

Flans, Robyn. "Labor of Love: A Salute to Fan Club Presidents," *Country Fever* (May/June 1995), 20-22.

Halbersberg, Elianne. "Pick Hit," Country Song Roundup (October 1995), 20-21.

Halbersberg, Elianne. "Silent Witness," *Country Song Roundup* (October 1995), 44.

Hemphill, Paul. *The Nashville Sound: Bright Lights and Country Music* (New York: Simon and Schuster, 1970).

Jackson, J.M. "Country Songwriter Spotlight," *Country Song Roundup* (October 1995), 36-39.

Jensen, Joli. "Honky-Tonking: Mass Mediated Culture Made Personal," in *All That Glitters,* ed. George H. Lewis (Bowling Green, Ohio: Bowling Green University Popular Press, 1993), 118-130.

Jensen, Joli. "Patsy Cline, Musical Negotiation and the Nashville Sound" in *All That Glitters,* ed. George H. Lewis (Bowling Green, Ohio: Bowling Green University Popular Press, 1993), 38-50.

Jones, Margaret. *The Life and Times of Patsy Cline* (New York: HarperCollins Publishers, 1994).

Leppert, Richard and George Lipsitz. "Age, the Body and Experience in the Music of Hank Williams," in *All That Glitters,* ed. George H. Lewis (Bowling Green, Ohio: Bowling Green University Popular Press, 1993), 22-37.

Lewis, George H. "Tension, Conflict and Contradiction in Country Music," in *All That Glitters,* ed. George H. Lewis (Bowling Green, Ohio: Bowling Green University Popular Press, 1993), 208-220.

Malone, Bill C. *Southern Music. American Music.* (Lexington, Kentucky: The University Press of Kentucky, 1979).

McCall, Michael. "Emmylou Harris: Playing Musical Chairs," *Country Song Roundup* (October 1995), 58-59.

Oermann, Robert K. "Radio Barn Dances," *Music City News* (June 1995), 42-48.

Price, Deborah Evans. "Country Beat," *Country Song Roundup* (October 1995), 6-10.

Pugh, John. "Ernest Tubb: Country Music's Great White Father," *Music City News* (October 1971), 7.

Robertson, William. *k. d. lang* (Ontario, Canada: ECW Press, 1992).

Rogers, Jimmie N. *The Country Music Message: Revisited* (Fayettevillle, Arkansas: University of Arkansas Press, 1989).

Rogers, Jimmie N. and Stephen A. Smith, "Country Music and Organized Religion," in *All That Glitters,* ed. George H. Lewis (Bowling Green, Ohio: Bowling Green University Popular Press, 1993), 270- 284.

Rose, Van. "David Ball: A Long Time Coming," *Country Song Roundup* (October 1995), 26-28.

[Stuart, Marty]. "Marty Stuart: In His Own Words," *Country Song Roundup* (October 1995), 54.

Williams, Jr., Hank and Michael Bane. *Living Proof* (New York: G.P. Putnam's Sons, 1979).

Wing, Eliza. "Country's Unlikely Star," *Rolling Stone* (March 11, 1991).

Notes

1. Elizabeth Peters, *Naked Once More* (New York: Warner Books, 1989) page 26.

2. Roxanne Waggoner, music director, Brown Country Music Church, Nashville, Indiana. Personal letter, July 12, 1995.

3. S.A.J. Bradley, trans. and ed., *Anglo-Saxon Poetry* (Rutland, Vermont: Charles E. Tuttle, Co., 1982), page iv.

4. David Bryant, music programmer, WDAF-61 Country, Kansas City, Missouri. Personal interview, June 19, 1995.

5. Peg Brinkhoff, "Cow Camp Chronicles," *Country America* (July/August 1995), page 64.

6. "Hillbilly Hell" by Bob McDill and Wayland Holyfield, Bibo Music Publishers, 1976.

7. Jimmie N. Rogers, *The Country Music Message: Revisited* (Fayetteville, Arkansas: University of Arkansas Press, 1989), page 38.

8. This quote and others can be seen displayed on the wall at the Country Music Foundation Hall of Fame in Nashville, Tennessee.

9. Paul Hemphill, *The Nashville Sound: Bright Lights and Country Music* (New York: Simon and Schuster, 1970), page 70.

10. This quote and others can be seen displayed on the wall at the Country Music Foundation Hall of Fame in Nashville, Tennessee.

11. Betsy Bowden, *Performed Literature: Words and Music by Bob Dylan* (Bloomington, Indiana: Indiana University Press, 1982), page 3.

12. Deborah Evans Price, "Country Beat," *Country Song Roundup* (October 1995), page 8.

13. Bradley, op. cit., page iv.

14. Hemphill, op. cit., pages 58-9.

15. Bill C. Malone, *Southern Music, American Music.* (Lexington, Kentucky: The University of Kentucky Press, 1979), page 63.

16. Robert K. Oermann, "Radio Barn Dances," *Music City News* (June 1995), page 43.

17. Curtis W. Ellison, *Country Music Culture* (Jackson, Mississippi: University of Mississippi Press, 1995), page 10.

18. George H. Lewis, "Tension, Conflict and Contradiction in Country Music," in *All That Glitters,* ed. George H. Lewis (Bowling Green, Ohio: Bowling Green University Popular Press, 1993) page 208.

19. Arline Chandler, "Making Mountain Music," *Country America* (May 1995), page 52.

20. Ibid., page 53.

21. James C. Cobb, "Country Music and the 'Southernization' of America," in *All That Glitters,* op. cit., page 75.

22. Jimmie N. Rogers, op. cit., page 163.

23. "Country Beat," *Country America* (July 1995), page 118.

24. Robyn Flans, "Corporate Country: Who's Sponsoring the Hot Summer Tours?" *Country Fever* (August 1995), page 27.

25. "Country Beat," op. cit., page 118.

26. Erma Bombeck, St Paul (Minnesota) *Pioneer Press,* July 9, 1995.

27. Bob Allen, "Twenty Questions With Tim McGraw," *Country Music* (July 1995), page 16.

28. David Bryant, op. cit.

29. *The New York Times,* August 15, 1995.

30. Elianne Halbersberg, "Pick Hit," *Country Song Roundup* (October 1995), pages 20-21.

31. Van Rose, "David Ball: A Long Time Coming," *Country Song Roundup* (October 1995), page 26.

32. David Bryant, op. cit.

33. Hank Williams, Jr and Michael Bane, *Living Proof* (New York: G.P. Putnam's Sons, 1979), page 10.

34. Ibid., page 12.

35. Ted Cramer, program director, WDAF-61 Country, Kansas City, Missouri. Personal interview, June 19, 1995.

36. J.M. Jackson, "Country Songwriter Spotlight," *Country Song Roundup* (October 1995), page 36.

37. Bob Ehlert, "Readin' and Writin' Coun-

try Music," *Country America* (July 1995), pages 77-78.

38. David Bryant, op. cit.,

39. Valerie Clark, "Fan Clubs: What to Expect," *Cross Country* (June 1995), page 14.

40. Robyn Flans, "Labor of Love: A Salute to Fan Club Presidents," *Country Fever* (May/June 1995), page 20.

41. Ibid., page 21.

42. Lawrence (Kansas) *Journal-World,* May 18, 1995.

43. "Letters," *Country America* (July 1995), page 16.

44. "Feedback," *Country Fever* (August 1995), page 5.

45. "Newsletter of the Country Music Society of America," *Country Music* (July/August 1995), page E.

46. Ibid., page E.

47. "Letters," *Country Music* (July 1995), page 60.

48. Ibid., page 58.

49. This set of stamps, issued in 1993, reproduced and significantly enlarged, can be seen on display at the Country Music Foundation Hall of Fame in Nashville, Tennessee. Others in the set include Patsy Cline, the Carter Family and Bob Wills.

50. "Marty Stuart: In His Own Words," *Country Song Roundup* (October 1995), page 54.

51. Margaret Jones, *The Life and Times of Patsy Cline* (New York: HarperCollins Publishers, 1994), page 10.

52. Ibid., page 244.

53. Ibid., page viii.

54. Ibid., page xiv.

55. Joli Jensen, "Patsy Cline, Musical Negotiation and the Nashville Sound," in *All That Glitters,* op. cit., page 46.

56. Charles T. Brown, *Music U. S. A.* (Englewood Cliffs, New Jersey: Prentice-Hall), page 150.

57. Hemphill, op. cit. page 236.

58. Ibid., page 236-7.

59. Ibid., page 237.

60. Bowden, op. cit. page 8.

61. Houston (Texas) *Chronicle,* August 7, 1990.

62. Bowden, op. cit., page 27.

63. Ibid., page 7.

64. Ibid., page 2.

65. Ibid., page 27.

66. *Los Angeles Times,* October 17, 1993.

67. Mary A. Bufwack and Robert K. Oermann, *Finding Her Voice. The Saga of Women in Country Music* (New York: Crown Publishers, Inc., 1993), page 423.

68. Ibid., page 425.

69. Pittsburgh (Pennsylvania) *Press,* December 10, 1988.

70. *Staten Island Advance,* August 2, 1989.

71. *The Washington Post,* March 15, 1992.

72. *Los Angeles Times,* October 17, 1993.

73. Michael McCall, "Emmylou Harris: Playing Musical Chairs," *Country Song Roundup* (October 1995), pages 58-59.

74. New York *Journal News,* February 22, 1990.

75. William Robertson, *k. d. lang* (Ontario: ECW Press, 1992), page 66.

76. *USA Today,* April 26, 1988.

77. Salinas *Californian,* January 17, 1990.

78. New York *Journal News,* op. cit.

79. John Pugh, "Ernest Tubb: Country Music's Great White Father," *Music City News* (October 1971), page 7.

80. Nashville *Banner,* September 16, 1984.

81. Salinas *Californian,* op. cit.

82. Ibid.

83. "Music Reviews," *Country America* (July/August 1995), page 120.

84. Cobb, op. cit., page 77.

85. Junior O'Quinn, President of the Hank Williams Fan Club, Personal interview, June 22, 1995.

86. Ibid.

87. Nashville *Banner,* October 20, 1986.

88. Providence (Rhode Island) *Bulletin,* October 29, 1990.

89. New York *Post,* December 27, 1992.

90. Erie (Pennsylvania) *Times,* April 24, 1986.

91. Providence (Rhode Island) *Bulletin,* op. cit.

92. Williamsport (Pennsylvania) *Sun Gazette,* April 21, 1984.

93. Richard Leppert and George Lipsitz, "Age, the Body and Experience in the Music of Hank Williams," in *All That Glitters,* op. cit., page 22.

94. Ellison, op. cit., page 73.

95. Ibid., page 76.

96. Leppert and Lipsitz, op. cit., page 22.

97. Ibid., page 34.

98. Bufwack and Oermann, op. cit., page 406.

99. El Centro (California) *Imperial Valley Press,* February 26, 1990.

100. Bufwack and Oermann, op. cit., page 450.

101. Ibid., page 406.

102. Everett (Washington) *Herald,* August 16, 1992.

103. Bufwack and Oermann, op. cit. page 534.

104. Palm Beach (Florida) *Sun Sentinel,* October 17, 1986.

105. Everett (Washington) *Herald,* op. cit.

106. Milwaukee (Wisconsin) *Journal,* August 10, 1988.

107. Birmingham (Alabama) *News,* March 1, 1992.

108. *U. S. A. Today,* August 12, 1994.

109. The Nashville *Tennessean,* July 14, 1995.

110. Jimmie N. Rogers and Stephen A. Smith, "Country Music and Organized Religion," in *All That Glitters,* op. cit., page 271.

111. Elianne Halbersberg, "Silent Witness," *Country Song Roundup* (October 1995), page 44.

112. Roxanne Waggoner, op. cit.

113. New York *Post,* October 16, 1974.

114. Halbersberg, op. cit., page 44.

115. Ibid., page 44.

116. Ibid., page 44.

117. San Antonio (Texas) *Express News,* February 20, 1988.

118. Freeport (Illinois) *Journal Standard,* September 17/18, 1988.

119. Williams, Jr. and Bane, op. cit., page 64.

120. Ibid., page 262.

121. Ibid., page 52.

122. Ibid., page 53.

123. Ibid., page 52.

124. Ibid., page 53.

125. Luray (Virginia) *Courier,* June 21, 1990.

126. Jackson (Tennessee) *Sun,* September 2, 1990.

127. Lancaster (Pennsylvania) *New Era,* August 23, 1990.

128. Luray (Virginia) *Courier,* op. cit.

129. Ibid.

130. Pittsburgh (Pennsylvania) *Press,* November 1, 1990.

131. Eliza Wing, "Country's Unlikely Star," *Rolling Stone* (March 11, 1991).

132. Steve Dougherty and Marge Sellinger, "Urbane Cowgirl Blues," *People* (August 31, 1992).

133. *The New York Times,* August 9, 1992.

134. *Country Song Roundup* (October 1995), page 82.

135. "The World of Country Music," *Music City News* (June 1995), page 86.

136. Ibid.

137. Birmingham (Alabama) *News,* July 7, 1989.

138. "The World of Country Music," op. cit., page 87.

139. St. Paul (Minnesota) *Pioneer Press,* June 5, 1995.

140. Providence (Rhode Island) *The Newspaper,* March 15, 1990.

141. Phoenix (Arizona) *Republic,* January 25, 1991.

142. Chicago (Illinois) *Reader,* December 10, 1982.

143. Lee's Summit (Missouri) *Journal,* October 7, 1988.

144. Phoenix (Arizona) *Republic,* January 25, 1991.

145. Boston (Massachusetts) *Herald,* October 18, 1990.

146. Atlanta (Georgia) *Journal,* July 13, 1989.

147. Clarksburg (West Virginia) *Telegram,* February 2, 1990.

148. Lincoln (Nebraska) *Journal,* November 8, 1990.

149. "Garth Brooks: In His Own Words," *Country Song Roundup* (October 1995), page 5.

150. This and other following Garth Brooks' comments are from Garth Brooks, *The Hits,* CD liner notes (Nashville: Liberty Records, 1995.)

❀

Notes

Index